THE SEVEN
BLUNDERS OF THE PEAK

THE SEVEN
BLUNDERS OF THE PEAK

A re-appraisal and exposition of some of the myths
and legends of the Peak District

Compiled and edited by

Brian Robinson

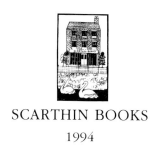

SCARTHIN BOOKS
1994

Design: Ivan Sendall

Phototypesetting: Paragon Typesetters, Deeside

Printing: Redwood Books, Wiltshire

Published by Scarthin Books, Cromford, Derbyshire 1994

ISBN 0 907758 77 0

'Man is a credulous animal, and must believe *something*; in the absence of good grounds for belief, he will be satisfied with bad ones'.

Bertrand Russell (1892-1970), in *Unpopular Essays* (1950), 'Outline of Intellectual Rubbish'.

'A myth is, of course, not a fairy story. It is the presentation of facts belonging to one category in the idioms appropriate to another. To explode a myth is accordingly not to deny the facts but to re-allocate them. And this is what I am trying to do.'

Gilbert Ryle (1900-1976), British philosopher, in the introduction to *Concept of Mind* (1949).

Contents

DEDICATION

To M, with whom this book would not have been possible.

Preface

THE PEAK DISTRICT: GEOGRAPHICALLY AND etymologically the very name itself is an example of a perpetuated misconception, the *raison d'etre* of this book. The District is often identified with the Peak National Park, erroneously, because the latter excludes considerable areas of it, mainly since they were already marred by industrialisation, especially the quarrying of limestone (which now, indeed, also defaces many areas *within* the Park). The most notable such omission is the long narrow enclave which bites into the Park from New Mills in the west and which includes Chapel-en-le-Frith and Buxton. Glossop is also excluded in the west, as are Matlock, Cromford and Wirksworth in the south-west and Ashbourne to the south. Furthermore, the Park is often regarded as being synonymous with the northern and western areas of Derbyshire, with a concomitant failure to appreciate that only just over half of it lies within that county, the remainder being found in the counties of Staffordshire and Cheshire and the metropolitan counties of South Yorkshire, West Yorkshire and Greater Manchester.

However, it is not only the confines but the very name itself that evokes a misconception when its etymology is attributed to some pointed summit; a mini-Matterhorn in a sort of mini-Alpine area at the southern end of the Pennine Chain. Indeed, such an image is portrayed in the seventeenth-century maps of the county – for example, those by Johann Blaeu (1645), Richard Blome (1681), Jan Jansson (1646) and John Speed (1611), all of which show the north-western tracts of the county liberally bestowed with quixotic peaks. Moreover, among many other perpetrators of the fallacy, Miss Mary Andrews begins her *Long Ago in Peakland* with the words 'Our Peakland is a land of mountains' and reinforces this with an illustration from the appropriate section of one of the early maps. In fact nothing could be further from the truth. Although the region's northern-most stretches do, in places, lie at just about 2,000 feet, they consist of the boggy moorland plateaus of Bleaklow and Kinder Scout: not a peak, in the sense of a sharply-pointed hill, anywhere. Indeed, to anyone with first-hand experience of these wastelands, 'Peat' District may spring to mind as a more appropriate name. The few bumps on the relevant section of the

earth's crust that do approach the shape of peaks lie just to the
south. The higher of these are manifest in Mam Tor, Lose Hill
and Win Hill, but the summits of all three are only about 1,500
feet above sea-level: at just less than half the altitudes, they are
hardly Snowdons or Scafells!

It would appear that the name was derived in the first place
from the people or tribe who occupied the territory thereabouts, the northernmost limit of the Saxon kingdom of Mercia,
in the seventh century. The first reference to these dwellers, in
a contemporary Saxon record, the *Tribal Hedage*, refers to them
as 'Pecsaetna'. 'Saete' or 'saetan' is an old English word for
'dwellers' and 'Pec' may be likewise derived from 'peac', meaning a hill, but not necessarily a high or pointed one. So the Pecsaetna, it would appear, were the 'hill-dwellers'. Alternatively,
according to Eilert Ekwall in *The Concise Oxford Dictionary of
English Place-Names*, 'peac' may be related to a Dutch word
meaning 'a dagger', a Swedish word meaning 'a cudgel', a
Norwegian word meaning 'a stick', and presumably an English
word meaning 'a pick'. Thus, is it too fanciful to suggest that the
Pecsaetna could just as easily have been the people who carried
daggers, cudgels or sticks?

In the *Anglo-Saxon Chronicle*, under the year 924, the region is
referred to as 'Peaclond', which should be interpreted as the
'land of the hill-dwellers' – if not, of the 'dagger/cudgel/stick
carriers'. However, by the end of the twelfth century either the
hill had become a mountain (peak) or the original name had
been forgotten and 'Pec' or 'Peac' had phonetically evolved
accordingly, for by this time the region had become known as
The Peak, a form popularised in the early nineteenth century by
Sir Walter Scott in his novel *Peveril of the Peak*. A comparatively
modern addition to the name is 'District' and this, more than
anything, has created the false impression of a 'district of peaks'.
Perhaps the intermediate name of Peakland, despite its
somewhat literary flavour, would have been an appropriate
stage at which to arrest the etymology.

Vested interests often prevail in the preservation of local
myths and fables, many of which have evolved around either
the Establishment, in its various guises, or the so-called prominent personages in a pseudo-feudal environment. Furthermore,
since times immemorial a fine legend or myth, which may
impart a sense of continuity and belonging, has always been
enjoyed; where there wasn't one, invention would often come
to the rescue. Such tales frequently arose by the unwitting
elaboration, with the passage of time, of a local past event or
artifact, sometimes thereby concealing a truth that is more

interesting as well as more credible. Legends with the romantic and moral overtones that appealed deeply to the Victorians abound, often being penned and embellished by local, and usually sycophantic, writers of this period. Furthermore, much recent literature relating to local history has either remained uncritical of such fanciful ramblings and nonsenses or, worse still, has actively perpetuated them, apparently adopting the philosophy underlying the Italian maxim 'se non e vero, e ben trovato' (if it's not true then it ought to be).

Charged with the offence of preserving or inventing mythical and legendary nonsenses in this way, a large quantity of the literature appertaining to the County of Derbyshire, and in particular its Peak District, would stand well and truly convicted. Indeed, a re-examination of the area's popular myths and legends and their banal and often embellished regurgitations is long overdue. The Peak has enough of true and genuine interest and can do without such absurdities.

Fortunately, indiscriminate and uncritical acceptance of folklore and legend has not been universal. Occasionally, the results of careful and erudite analysis have appeared in scholastic publications and in the periodicals of learned societies. Paramount amongst the latter is the *Journal of the Derbyshire Archaeological and Natural History Society*, published annually since 1879 (known as the *Derbyshire Archaeological Journal* since 1961).

Castleton Cavern.

Although such works are generally available, the public is largely unaware of their existence and may sometimes find their style forbidding. Hopefully, the present anthology of constructive criticism and evaluation will distinguish between fact, misconception, make-believe and error in some of the legends and myths of the Peak District. This collection is only the beginning!

This present 'debunking' is, however, far from the first. It was, perhaps, the pioneer journalist and novelist Daniel Defoe who, as part of his work *A Tour thro' the Whole Island of Great Britain*, which first appeared in instalments between 1724 and 1726, first laid low a Peak District myth. This involved his classic debunking of the so called 'Seven Wonders of the Peak' which had been contrived by Thomas Hobbes in 1636 – although conceived fourteen years earlier by Michael Drayton – and further elaborated by Charles Cotton in 1681.

It is therefore appropriate to call on the spirit of Daniel Defoe to furnish the first chapter of this book. I cannot thank Daniel, but I should like to express my thanks to all the other contributors and to Dr David Mitchell, our courageous publisher, for all his help and advice. It has been my great pleasure to have been granted the privilege of leading such a fine team.

Brian Robinson, Eyam, Derbyshire
May 1994

Contributors

Julie Bunting, Goss Hall, Ashover, Chesterfield, Derbyshire, S45 0JN.
Together with her family, Julie Bunting shares interests in the countryside, local history and travel, subjects which have led her into an established literary career. She has written a number of books and a wide variety of features for national magazines, in addition to the numerous articles which for some years she has been contributing to the *Peak Advertiser*.

Harry E Butterton, 37 Windley Crescent, Darley Abbey, Derby, DE22 1BY.
Harry Butterton taught for seventeen years in secondary and comprehensive schools, mainly in the south of England, before coming north to take charge of St Helen's House in Derby for two years. From 1975 until his retirement at the end of 1990 he was successively Humanities and County History Adviser for Derbyshire Education Committee. Since retirement, he has written four books on aspects of Derby's nineteenth century history, including *Derby: From Regency to Golden Jubilee*, published last year. He is at present working on a two-volume study of the Derby Victorians based on the county's most notable newspaper, the *Derby Mercury*.

Daniel Defoe, (late of) Stoke Newington.

Peter Gilbert, B.Sc., Ph.D., The University of Manchester, Manchester, M13 9PL.
Dr Peter Gilbert graduated in Bacteriology from the University of Newcastle in 1972 and gained his doctorate in Microbial Physiology in 1975. Following the tenure of a postdoctoral research fellowship at the University of Aston, during which he investigated bacterial resistance to antibiotics, he was in 1978 appointed to a lectureship at the University of Manchester where, in 1989, he was promoted to Senior Lecturer. He has researched and published widely on microbial physiology, infectious disease and antibiotic resistance, on which subjects he has published over two hundred learned articles in books and scientific journals.

P R Ineson, B.Sc., Ph.D., D.Sc., C.Eng., F.I.M.M., F.G.S., Department of Earth Sciences, The University of Sheffield, Sheffield, S3 7HF.
Eur Ing P R Ineson has some twenty-five years' experience in the fluorspar industry. After initially undertaking research work on the deposits in the UK Pennines, Spain, USA and Poland he joined Laporte Industries Ltd at their Cavendish Mill, Eyam, Derbyshire, as a Research Officer. He subsequently joined the University of Sheffield and has published numerous professional research papers and industrial articles on fluorspar and the related minerals. Consultancies related to the mining and exploration for fluorspar are also ongoing. He has been a Jury Member of the Barmote Court for some twenty years.

Richard M Litchfield, B.Ed., 16 Jackson Road, Matlock, Derbyshire, DE2 3JQ.
Richard Litchfield is currently teaching English at Tupton Hall Comprehensive School, near Chesterfield. He is deeply interested in the local history and folklore of the Peak, and has written three books with a local theme: *A Dog Called Badger, Badger, More Tales of a Peakland Pooch*, and *Strange Tales of the Peak*, the two latter being available in the Derbyshire Heritage series. He is also interested in the Old West, and his two novels about the railroad detective and gunman, Tom Blood, *Blood Will Have Blood* and *Blood in Paradise* are published by Robert Hale.

Brian Robinson, M.Sc., Ph.D., D.Sc., F.R.S.C., 'Millhaven', Tideswell Lane, Eyam, Derbyshire, S30 1RD.
During the tenure of a succession of academic appointments – at the Universities of Illinois (Chicago), Kumasi (Ghana), Manchester, Naples, Nottingham, Sassari (Sardinia) and St Andrews – Dr Brian Robinson has published some one hundred original research papers in the areas of organo-medicinal chemistry and molecular pharmacology and his scientific magnum opus *The Fischer Indole Synthesis* (Wiley; 1982). He has also made literary contributions to numismatics, including two books – *The Royal Maundy* (Kaye and Ward; 1977) and *Silver Pennies and linen towels: the story of the Royal Maundy* (Spink; 1992), and to Derbyshire's industrial archaelogy by his books *Birchinlee, the workmen's village of the Derwent Valley Water Board* (1983) and *Walls across the valley. The building of the Howden and Derwent Dams* (Scarthin Books; 1993).

Roland Smith, 33 Park Road, Bakewell, Derbyshire.
Roland Smith is Head of Information Services to the Peak National Park and an award-winning journalist and author. He has written twelve books about the British countryside and walking, including the best-selling *Wildest Britain* (Blandford Press; 1983), and most recently *Explore Britain's National Parks* (AA Publishing; 1993) and *On Foot in the Pennines* (David and Charles; 1994). He came to the National Park ten years ago, after a twenty-year career in daily paper journalism during which he was Fisons Agricultural Journalist of the Year in 1983. For the past five years he has been chairman of the Outdoor Writers' Guild, and contributes regularly to most outdoor magazines.

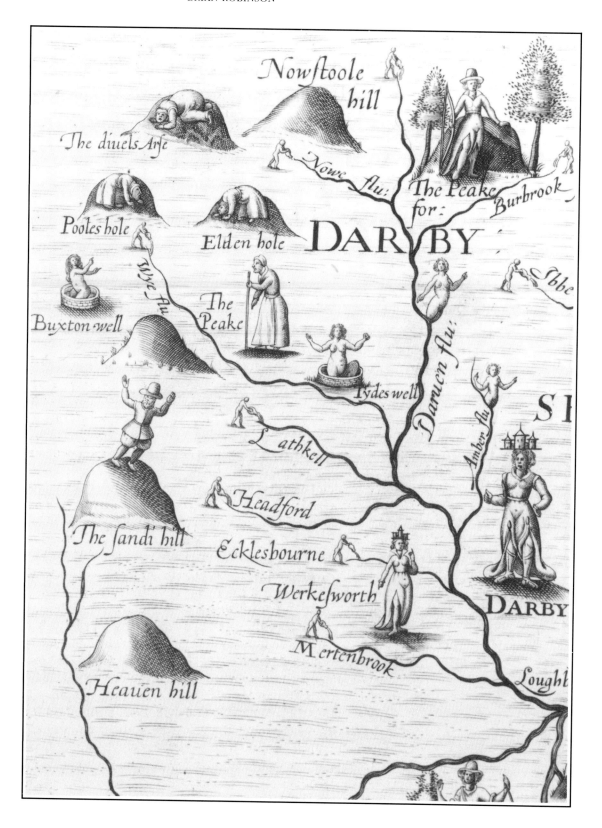

CHAPTER 1

The Seven (Wonderless) Wonders of The Peak

by Daniel Defoe and, in part, Brian Robinson

MICHAEL DRAYTON, THE SON OF A LOCAL butcher, was born at Hartshill, near Atherstone in Warwickshire, in 1563. As a page he entered the service of Sir Henry Goodere, of Powlesworth, who was largely responsible for his employee's education and the encouragement of his literary ability – he became a friend of William Shakespeare and enjoyed, during the reigns of Elizabeth I and James I, a considerable reputation as a poet. He died in London on 23 December 1631 and was buried in Westminster Abbey, where a statue was erected by the Countess of Dorset to the memory of '. . . the modest and amiable man'.

Drayton's main work first appeared in 1612 under the title *Poly-Olbion*, but in the second edition, which appeared in the following year, this had been expanded to *Poly-Olbion Or a Chorographicall Description of Tracts, Rivers, Mountaines, Forests, and other Parts of this renowned Isle of Great Britaine* . . . The texts of both these works were the same, namely eighteen poems each immediately preceded by an appropriate allegorical illustrative map, these latter probably being engraved by William Hole. However, none of the poems covers the area of Derbyshire, although this omission was rectified in a third, and final, edition that was published in 1622. It was printed in two parts, the first embodying the texts and maps in the edition of 1613 and the second twelve new 'songs' (poems), and ten new maps. The eighth new 'song', 'The sixe and twentieth Song', and its related map (Figure 1), covers the areas of 'Nottingham Shyre', 'Lecester Shyre' and 'Darby Shyre', with the last county's portrayal consisting in the main of a lyrical exposition of the 'Peake' and its 'Seven wonders' – as delineated by Drayton, these were 'The Divels-Arse' [Peak Cavern, Castleton] (Figure 2), 'Poole's

Figure 2. The Devil's Arse (Peak Cavern, Castleton) as portrayed with the map of Derbyshire by Herman Moll in 1724.

Figure 3. Poole's Hole (Poole's Cavern, Buxton) as portrayed with the map of Derbyshire by Herman Moll in 1724.

Hole' [Poole's Cavern, Buxton] (Figure 3), 'Elden Hole', 'Saint Anne of Buckston' [St Anne's Well, Buxton] (Figure 4), 'Tydeswell' [the ebbing-and-flowing well – at Tideswell or Barmoor Clough (*vide infra*)?], 'Sandy (Sandi) Hill' [Mam Tor, the so-called 'shivering mountain', at Castleton] and 'The Peake Forrest'.

William Camden, in his *Britannia*, the classical work, which first appeared in 1586, on the history of Britain from pre-Roman times, makes mention of only three 'Wonders' – which clearly failed to impress him – in the Peak when he writes:

'Mira alto Pecco tria sunt, barathrum, specus, antrum;
Commoda tot, Plumbum, Gramen, Ovile pecus.
Tot speciosa simul sunt, Castrum, Balnea, Chatsworth,
Plura sed occurrunt, quae speciosa minus.'
[Nine Things that please us at the Peak we see;
A Cave, a Den, a Hole, the Wonder be;
Lead, Sheep and Pasture, are the useful Three.
Chatsworth the Castle, and the Bath delight,
Much more you see; all little worth the Sight].

Thus, in the absence of intervening literature, it would appear that the concept of the 'Seven Wonders of the Peak' belongs to Drayton. Sadly, however, this fact has, until now, gone unrecognised by the many who have written about them and who have erroneously ascribed their genesis to Thomas Hobbes' poem *De Mirabilibus Pecci* (Concerning the Wonders of the Peak) which, written in Latin hexameters, first appeared in 1636, namely fourteen years *after* the appearance of Drayton's conceptual work. Indeed, Hobbes himself makes no reference to or acknowledgement of the earlier work, although he must have made use of it for his seven 'Wonders', with one significant modification (*vide infra*), are identical with those of Drayton – hardly coincidental!

Thomas Hobbes (Figure 5) was born at Malmesbury in 1588. The son of a vicar, he had the good fortune to be sent to Oxford University – how different from Drayton's early days – and to be appointed tutor to the Cavendish family, then by far the largest owners of land in the Peak and whose family home was then, as now, Chatsworth House. Among his literary works, Hobbes wrote in 1640 a defence of the royal prerogative which led to him fleeing the country for fear of the wrath of Parliament. Eleven years later, when he issued *Leviathan*, he incurred the hatred of the Royalists by urging obedience to whoever wielded effective supreme power – at that time Cromwell. Despite his ability to antagonise both sides in politics he

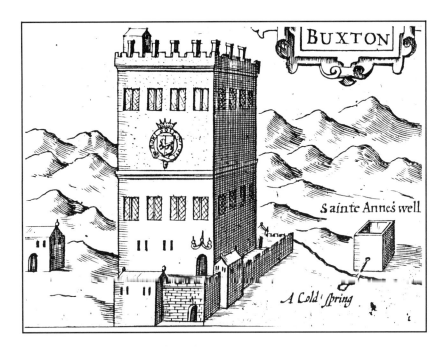

Figure 4. Sainte Anne's well (Buxton) as portrayed with the map of Derbyshire by John Speed in 1611.

Figure 5. Thomas Hobbes (1588-1679) reproduced by courtesy of the National Trust (Hardwick Hall) photography by the Courtauld Institute of Art (Somerset House, London).

he received at the age of sixty-five a life pension from the Cavendishes, supplemented by a generous annual allowance of £100 from the Crown. On these he lived a further twenty-six years, dying in 1679 at Hardwick, where his monument may be seen in the church.

His first literary effort was the poem *De Mirabilibus Pecci*, one of the early eulogies of the area which was no doubt imbued with patriotism and possibly even a vested interest in promoting the district. Hobbes summarised the wonders in one line, namely 'AEdes, Mons, Barathrum, binus Fons, Antraque bina' (House, mountain, pit, two fountains and two caves), referring to Chatsworth House, Mam Tor at Castleton, Eldon Hole, St Anne's Well in Buxton (Figure 4), the ebbing-and-flowing well in Barmoor Clough, Poole's Cavern in Buxton (Figure 3) and Peak Cavern in Castleton (Figure 2). Of these, all but Chatsworth House are natural features – indeed, six of the seven as previously elaborated by Drayton – and one wonders whether it was not a sycophantic Hobbes attempting to ingratiate himself with his patrons that prompted him not only to replace 'The Peake Forrest' of Drayton by Chatsworth House, but to place it first in his list of alleged wonders.

A similar theme to that of Hobbes was later exploited by Charles Cotton in *The Wonders of the Peak*, first published in 1681 and, like the earlier work, running into several editions. The wonders were the same and not only was Chatsworth House once again placed first but it was referred to in the following glowing terms:

'And one of them so singularly rare,
As does, indeed, amount to miracle,
And all the Kingdom boasts, so far excel.
It ought not, I confess, to be Profan'd
By my poor Muse; nor should an Artless Hand
Presume to take a Crayon up, to trace
But the faint Land-scape of so brave a Place.
Yet noble Chatsworth (for I speak of thee)
Pardon the Love will prompt the Injury
My pen must do thee, when before I end,
I fix Dishonour, where I should Commend.'

Further fawning is apparent from the work's dedication that reads 'To the Right Honourable Elizabeth Countess of Devonshire, this Essay is with all Acknowledgement and Devotion humbly Dedicated by Her Ladyship's Most Humble and Most Obedient Servant, Charles Cotton'. Certainly it was in Cotton's interest to curry the favour of the Cavendish family since, when he was not enjoying London society or hiding from his creditors, he lived at Beresford Hall in the heart of the nearby Dovedale.

However, although the so-called wonders were conceived and born out of obsequiousness, they were widely accepted by a credulous populace and later extolled by other writers. For example, prefaced by 'But that which renders the Peak most famous is what are generally called, The seven Wonders of the Peak', the verses of Hobbes (in Latin) and Cotton (in English) describing each of the seven wonders are quoted in their entirety in *Magna Britannia Antiqua & Nova* (1738) (pages 434-446), which accepts these features as wonders and adds, moreover, 'some other Rarities belonging to the Soil here' [Blue John, for example?]. Similarly, the wonders were accepted without comment or criticism by Rev. R Ward in his work some eight decades later, and have been regurgitated by others in contemporary and subsequent works, the latest being Merrill in 1993.

Unfortunately, none of these authors appears to be cognizant of Daniel Defoe's work *A Tour thro' the Whole Island of Great Britain*, which first appeared in print in instalments between 1724 and 1726 and in which he describes his journey through Derbyshire, including the Peak. Here, this superb debunker, scorning the worship of natural wonders, paid particular attention to those purported by Hobbes and Cotton, dismissing most of them with something approaching contempt.

Travelling northward from the south of the County, via Brassington Moor, Defoe describes his first encounter with a Hobbes' wonder as:

'Buxton Bath [St Anne's Well – Figure 4], which they call one of the Wonders of the Peak; but is so far from being a Wonder, that to us, who had been at Bath in Somersetshire, and at Aix la Chappelle in Germany, it was nothing at all; nor is it anything but what is frequent in such Mountainous Countries as this is, in many Parts of the World.

That which was more wonderful to me than all of it, was, that so light is made of them as to Use; that the People rather wonder at them than take the Benefit [allegedly curative] of them; and that, as there are several hot Springs in this Village of Buxton, as well as Matlock, mentioned above, and at several other Places, they are not built into noble and convenient bathing Places; and, instead of a House or two, a City built here for the Entertainment of Company; which, if it were done, and Countenance given to it, as is to the Baths at Bath, I doubt not it would be as well frequented, and to as good purpose [perhaps the later developers of Buxton and Matlock as spas took Defoe's suggestions to heart].

But though I shall not treat this warm Spring as a Wonder, for such it is not; I must nevertheless give it the Praise due to the medicinal Virtue of its Waters; for it is not to be deny'd, but that wonderful Cures have been wrought by them, especially in Rheumatick, Scorbutick and scrofulous Distempers, Aches of the Joints, nervous Pains, and also in scurfy and leprous Maladies.'

He concludes:

'Of Buxton; the Wonder to me is, that in a Nation so full of Chronical Diseases as we are, such as our Scorbuticks, Rheumaticks, Cholicks and Niphriticks, there should be such a Fountain of Medicine sent from Heaven, and no more notice taken of it, or care to make it useful.'

Still in Buxton, Defoe encountered the second wonder which he summarily dismissed as 'a great Cave or Hole in the Earth, called Poole's Hole [Poole's Cavern – Figure 3], another of the Wonderless Wonders of the Peak' and later added 'in short, there is nothing in Poole's Hole to make a Wonder of, any more than as other Things in Nature, which are rare to be seen, however easily accounted for, may be called wonderful'. Then, after elaborating a legend concerning the cavern, he concluded 'This helps among the People there, to make out the Wonder; and indeed such things are wanting where really Wonder is wanting, else there would be no wonder at all in it; as indeed there is not'.

In a different way, Defoe was equally dismissive in his description of Mam Tor:

'or, as the Word in the Mountain Jargon signifies, the Mother Rock, upon a Suggestion that the soft crumbling Earth, which falls from the Summit of the one, breeds or begets several young Mountains below. The Sum of the Wonder is this, That there is a very high Hill, nay, I will add (that I may make the most of the Story, and that it may appear as much like a Wonder as I can) an exceedingly high Hill. But this in a Country which is all over Hills, cannot be much of a Wonder, because also there are several higher Hills in the Peak than that, only not just there.

The South Side of this Hill is a Precipice, and very steep from the Top to the Bottom; and as the Substance of this Hill is not a solid Stone, or rocky, as is the Case of all the Hills thereabouts, but a crumbling loose Earth mingled with small Stones, it is continually falling down in small Quantities, as the force of hasty Showers, or solid heavy Rains, loosens and washes it off, or as Frosts and Thaws operate upon it in common with other Parts of the Earth; now as the great Hill, which is thick, as well as high, parts with this loose Stuff, without being sensibly diminished, yet the bottom which it falls into, is more easily perceived to swell with the Quantity that falls down; the Space where it is received being small, comparatively to the height and thickness of the Mountain: Here the pretended Wonder is form'd, namely, that the little Heap below, should grow up into a Hill, and yet the great Hill not be the less for all that is fallen down; which is not true in fact, any more than, as a great black Cloud pouring down Rain as it passes over our Heads, appears still as great and as black as before, though it continues pouring down rain over all the Country. But nothing is more certain than this, that the more Water comes down from it, the less remains in it; and so it certainly is of Mam Tor, in spite of all the Poetry of Mr Cotton or Mr Hobbes, and in spite of all the Women's Tales in the Peak.'

Our tourist soon came upon the next professed wonder, Peak Cavern, for he resumes:

'This Hill [Mam Tor] lies on the North Side of the Road from Buxton to Castleton, where we come to the so famed Wonder call'd, saving our good Manners, The Devil's A____e in the Peak [Peak Cavern was contemporarily referred to as the Devil's Arse (Figure 2); in Domesday Book it receives the more functional title 'Pikserse']; Now notwithstanding the grossness of the Name given it, and that there is nothing of similitude or coherence either in Form and Figure, or any other thing between the thing signified and the thing signifying; yet we must search narrowly for any thing in it to make a Wonder, or even any thing so strange, or odd, or vulgar, as the Name would seem to import.'

And after further deliberation upon the cavern concluded 'we cannot think there is any room to call it a Wonder'.

After further reflection concerning Peak Cavern, Defoe proceeds:

'The next Wonder, which makes up Number five, is called Tideswell, or a Spring of Water which ebbs and flows, as they will have it, as the Sea does. A poor thing indeed to make a Wonder of; and therefore most of the Writers pass it over with little notice; only that they are at a loss to make up the Number seven without it'.

Defoe, in fact, inspected the wrong ebbing-and-flowing well, for the one referred to by both Hobbes and Cotton was situated on the roadside in Barmoor Clough, about half-a-mile south-west of Sparrowpit. However, it has long ceased to ebb-and-flow, probably because the subterranean siphon that caused this effect has either been destroyed or is permanently flooded by the small reservoir that has been formed on the side of the road almost directly opposite to it. Furthermore, it is doubtful that Defoe would have been any more impressed by the Barmoor Clough well than he was by that at Tideswell and, in any case, Derbyshire is not alone is possessing such geological features. For example, the River Tems rises at a notable ebbing-and-flowing well (*which still functions*) under the limestone of Giggleswick Scar, near Settle, in Yorkshire.

Defoe summarised his impressions thus far by stating 'So much for fictitious Wonders, or indeed simple Wonders' and concluding that to him a wonder was 'That in a Nation so curious, so inquiring, and so critical as this is, any thing so unsatisfying, so foolish and so weak, should pass for Wonders as those of Mam Tor, Tideswell, Poole's Hole, &c'. Nevertheless, he did appear to be impressed with Hobbes' two remaining entrants, Chatsworth House and Eldon Hole, though even his eulogy on Chatsworth appears to be somewhat tongue-in-cheek:

'If there is any Wonder in Chatsworth, it is, that any Man who had a Genius suitable to so magnificent a Design, who could lay out the Plan for such a House, and had a Fund to support the Charge, would build it in such a Place where the Mountains insult the Clouds, intercepting the Sun, and would threaten, were Earthquakes frequent here, to bury the very Towns, much more the House, in their Ruins'

and concludes that:

'As to Chatsworth, the Wonder, as I said before, seems to me; not that so noble and magnificent a Palace should be built, but that it should be built in such a Situation, and in such a Country so out of the way, so concealed from the World, that whoever sees it must take a Journey on purpose'.

It remained the sole prerogative of Eldon Hole to really impress Defoe when he wrote:

'The remaining Article, and which, I grant, we may justly call a WONDER, is Elden Hole: The Description of it, in brief, is thus: In the middle of a plain open Field, gently descending to the South, there is a frightful Chasme, or opening in the Earth, or rather in the Rock, for the Country seems thereabouts to be all but one great Rock; this opening goes directly down perpendicular into the Earth, and perhaps to the Center [the contemporary credulity would appear to have well and truly infected Defoe]; it may be about twenty Foot over one way, and fifty or sixty the other; it has no Bottom, that is to say, none that can yet be heard of. Mr Cotton says, he let down eight hundred Fathoms of Line into it, and that the Plummet drew still; so that, in a word, he sounded about a Mile perpendicular; for as we call a Mile 1760 Yards, and 884 is above half, then doubtless eight hundred Fathoms must be 1600 Yards, which is near a Mile.

This I allow to be a Wonder, and what the like of is not to be found in the World, that I have heard of, or believe. And would former Writers have been contented with one Wonder instead of seven, it would have done more Honour to the Peak, and even to the whole Nation, than the adding five imaginary Miracles to it that had nothing in them, and which really depreciated the whole.

Elden Hole I acknowledge to be a wonderful Place, as I have said above; but to me the greatest Surprize is, that, after such a real Wonder, any of the Trifles added to it could bear the Name of Wonders'.

However, one wonders for how long Defoe's wonder of Eldon Hole would have remained had he been aware of its relatively modest depth, as first established during the pioneering descent and exploration by John Lloyd, F.R.S., in June 1780. At some 245 feet it is well short of several Yorkshire chasms, notably Gaping Ghyll. The first recorded descent of this was by the Frenchman E A Martel, who took twenty-three minutes to reach the bottom, on Thursday, 1 August 1895. It falls 365 feet into a great chamber some 500 feet in length and some 80 feet wide.

In any case, for Defoe, a 'real' wonder was such as he himself discovered near Brassington Moor; a family living in a cave and consisting of a lead-miner, his wife and five children. Although the parents both worked hard, the family was only in receipt of a modest income, but, nevertheless, appeared to want for nothing and were very happy and content. Truly a WONDER – indeed, a timeless one so long as avarice and envy predominate as human characteristics, and one far removed from the publicity-seeking and favour-currying motives of Hobbes and Cotton.

BIBLIOGRAPHY

A Chorographicall Description of . . . Great Britain . . . , by Michael Drayton (Iohn Marriott, Iohn Grismand and Thomas Dewe; 1622), pp.115-127 (in particular pp.123-126 and the map immediately preceding p.115).

A guide to the Peak of Derbyshire, by Rev R Ward, 7th edition (where are the previous six editions?), (Birmingham, no date), p.171.

'An account of Elden Hole in Derbyshire', by J Lloyd; with some observations upon it, by Edward King, in *Philosophical Transactions of the Royal Society*, 1771, **61,** pp.250-265 + figures I-V.

A Tour thro' the Whole Island of Great Britain, by Daniel Defoe, (New impression of New edition), vol II (Frank Cass and Co Ltd, 1968), pp.562-587.

'De Mirabilibus Pecci', by Thomas Hobbes (in *The History, Gazetteer, and Directory of the County of Derby*, by Stephen Glover (1829), Appendix No 2, pp.9-19).

Derbyshire Folklore, by John N Merrill (Trail Crest Publications; 1993), pp.4-11.

Derbyshire, the Peak Country, ed. by Arthur Mee (Hodder and Stoughton, London; 1937), pp.32, 33.

Looking at old maps, by John Booth (Cambridge House Books, Westbury; 1970), pp.46-48.

Portrait of the Pennines, by Roger A Redfern (Robert Hale, London; 1971), p.68.

The Dictionary of National Biography (Oxford University Press), **6**, pp.8-13.

The Peak District, by Roy Christian (David and Charles, Newton Abbot; 1976), p.10.

The printed maps in the atlases of Great Britain and Ireland. A bibliography, 1579-1870, by Thomas Chubb (third impression) (Dawson, Folkestone; 1977), pp.45-47, 430, 433.

The Wonders of the Peake, by Charles Cotton, 4th edition (London, 1725), p.301.

Reference to the Unions

1 Glossop
2 Hayfield Part
3 Chapel en le Frith
4 Bakewell
5 Ecclesall Bierlow Part
6 Chesterfield
7 Rotherham Part
8 Worksop Part
9 Mansfield Part
10 Belper
11 Basford Part
12 Uttoxeter Part
13 Burton on Trent Part
14 Derby
15 Shardlow Part
16 Tamworth Part
17 Ashby de la Zouch Part
18 Ashbourne Part

DERBYSHIRE

CHAPTER 2

The Tale of
The Vanishing Captain
– The Birth and Demise
of a Myth

by Richard M Litchfield

THE STRENGTH AND RESILIENCE OF MYTHS SEEMS TO lie in their age. Most are so old and have evolved through so many tellings that it is virtually impossible to trace them to their point of origin and examine what proof there may be either for or against. Without definite, concrete evidence, the credulous listener merely shakes his head and says, 'Well, there must be something in it. My grandad told me . . . .'.

Whilst researching old murders in the Peak, however, I chanced across a myth that was still relatively young. I was able to follow it back, if not to its moment of conception then at least to the point where it took wing and flew out into the wide world.

It was a friend who put me on to it. Knowing that I was tentatively planning a book on unusual murders in the Peak, he said, 'You want to look at the case of the disappearing captain, at Eyam in the last century. It's an amazing story'.

The story, as my friend told it, was that an old man, a retired captain who had lived at Delf View in Eyam, had simply disappeared into thin air one night. He had fallen foul of some local leadminers, who had threatened his life. The captain, it was thought, had some sinister secret, or lived a double life, for he was to be seen late at night, riding a white horse through the countryside on some mysterious assignation. He was also a keen astronomer and liked on clear nights to observe the stars through his telescope from some high point outside the village, walking out alone and changing from his shoes to his boots on

A map of Derbyshire published by S. Lewis in the *Atlas to the Topographical Dictionary of England*, 1848.

29

a rock close by the house. One night, the story went, the captain did not return, and a search party later found his boots and telescope on the rock, but no sign of the man, no evidence of a struggle even, was found. The captain had quite simply disappeared, and was never seen again.

Heady stuff, and I knew that if the story could be authenticated it would make an intriguing chapter in my book. Also, I was bitten; I just had to know more! Some simple research at the Local Studies Library at County Offices in Matlock soon fleshed out the details of the story. In an old guide book to Eyam, published in 1947 and written by local historian Clarence Daniel, I came across the earliest reference to the tale my friend had told me. I found nothing new to add to it, save that some years earlier the captain had been involved in a mining tragedy in which some men had been suffocated, and that it was popularly supposed that leadminers had murdered the captain in an act of revenge and then hidden the body so successfully it was never found. It was all there, even the wonderfully gothic description of the captain riding through the night astride a white horse on some 'mysterious mission'.

A little digging in the archives showed that Delf View had indeed once been occupied by a captain, a Captain William Wyatt. I had originally assumed, however, that the captain of the mystery was a retired naval man, my assumption sparked subconsciously, I suppose, by the fact that, according to Clarence Daniel's account, he carried a telescope and had a knowledge of astronomy, both essential tools for maritime navigation. Wyatt's rank, though, was not a naval or even military one, but an honorific title, common in the mining industry in Cornwall for a surveyor or manager of a mine. Cornish miners were employed in the lead mines of the Peak, and several of the Wyatt family, including William's father, Benjamin, who were involved in the industry, had been accorded the title of 'Captain'.

Further research showed that William Wyatt had been involved in the 'Redsoil Murders' of 1833. A long-standing disagreement between the owners and miners of the Maypit and Redsoil Mines (to all intents and purposes the same mine and miners), and the Magpie Mine at Sheldon, near Bakewell, had been simmering for some years. The dispute was over rightful ownership of a vein of lead. Magpie miners following the vein had broken through into workings of the nearby Redsoil Mine, and feelings ran so high that the two groups of miners had been involved in fights below ground. Finally, in late August of 1833, both sides had caused fires to be lit underground to 'smoke' the other side out, and on Monday, September 2nd, Magpie men lit straw and either pitch or gas oil and caused it to be driven into the Redsoil workings. As a consequence, three men were overcome and killed by the noxious fumes.

At the subsequent inquest a verdict of wilful murder was returned against twenty of the Magpie miners, and John Green and William Wyatt, both part-owners of the mine, whom witnesses swore had either provided or known about the coal-oil and its intended use, were charged with being accessories before the fact. Seventeen of the miners were immediately arrested, but three others, along with Green and Wyatt, evaded arrest, saying that they would submit themselves for trial at Derby in six months' time.

At the trial it was shown that the Redsoil miners had begun the smoking some days earlier, and on the day of the tragedy the mine's agent, Henry Knowles, had ordered the Redsoil shafts to be covered, no doubt hoping to send the smoke from Magpie mine back on the Magpie miners. The smoke, however, had remained in the Redsoil workings, and Knowles had then, by force of threat, sent men below, saying that they must retain possession of the mine at all hazards, the consequence being that lives were lost in the poisoned air. All the accused were found not guilty, but the decision must have sat badly with the families and friends of the dead men. Their resentment would not have been helped by what could be seen as the gloating action of Wyatt, as reported in the *Derbyshire Courier* on Saturday, March 29th 1834:

'On Wednesday and Thursday last the ore carts of Mr William Wyatt conveyed the Magpie miners from Derby to Ashford. The horses attached to the vehicle were decorated with ribbons, bearing the motto "Truth and Justice".'

In the tight little local communities there must have been some who saw this unseemly celebration as crowing over the graves of the three men, and maybe threats were made against Wyatt which caused him to fear for his life.

So when, and more importantly how, did Wyatt die?

A cursory glance through books on Peak lead mining history, published by the Peak District Mines Historical Society, showed that Wyatt died in 1858, though there was no mention of his disappearance. The same publications showed that in his latter years Wyatt was afflicted with rheumatism and gout, frequently in pain and often bedridden (clearly not a man to go wandering abroad at night!). His mining ventures had nearly all failed, and he kept solvent by land deals, calf and lamb rearing and the smelting of lead. The writings showed that, even setting aside the Redsoil tragedy, he was not always a popular man, being parsimonious in his dealings with miners and lacking the technical expertise of other mine agents. He lost money on some ventures by installing wrong equipment or by not quitting early enough when it was clear that a mining venture was unprofitable. There is no clue to his personal character, though a Captain Wyatt is reported elsewhere to have horsewhipped Methodists in the streets of Tideswell. However, as others in the Wyatt family bore the same title of captain, perhaps this is more of an indicator of a family propensity towards violent conduct than an individual antipathy towards dissenters!

Given the year of 1858 as that of William Wyatt's death, it was only a matter of a little research in the newspapers of the time to turn up the captain's obituary, and with this the puzzle deepened, for the *Derbyshire Times* of Saturday, October 9th 1858 was quite definite on the subject:

'On Sunday last, at Foolow, near Tideswell, William Wyatt Esq, after a lingering illness. The above gentleman was agent to Lord Denman, Andrew Brittlebank Esq, and many others, besides being extensively connected with the mining operations of the county.'

So Wyatt died at home, at Foolow, not Eyam, in his bed, not at the hands of vengeful miners, but of a 'lingering illness'. The myth was exposed for what it was, a fanciful fiction, but how had it arisen?

If Wyatt had not disappeared from Delf View, and had not even been living there at the time of his death, then perhaps some other tenant of that place had been spirited away, and his name confused with that of the captain. Accordingly I turned to the files to see if there was anything written on the house itself, and soon discovered how the story first reached the ears of Clarence Daniel, and thus found its way into print.

In the February/March, 1957 edition, of the *Derbyshire Countryside* is an article by Daniel on Delf View. It deals mainly with the concert pianist Frederick Dawson, who lived at the Georgian mansion. Toward the end of the article, however, the author tells how, over twenty years ago, he had helped a lady from Chesterfield who had been researching her family tree. Amongst the many papers she showed him was one which told the story of Captain Wyatt – a relative of hers – and his mysterious disappearance whilst living at Delf View. The article gave the added information that Wyatt disappeared from the area above Middleton Dale, and the lady from Chesterfield who corresponded with Clarence Daniel suggested that a skeleton found the previous year in the dale might be that of her long-lost relative, adding that perhaps the captain had been eaten by wild animals! Daniel discounted the wild animal theory as highly unlikely, since there would be no animal at large in the last century which could pose such a danger, and anyway it would have left signs of a struggle for the search party to find. The bones found in Middleton Dale also proved to be even older than the plague (see Chapter 3), yet not prehistoric, and to be from a dozen different people, including children, posing yet another mystery.

The article on Delf View finished with Clarence Daniel saying that 'the fate of Capt. Wyatt remains an unsolved mystery; a secret with which only the stars are familiar, and which history will never know'.

History, if not the stars, had always known the answer to this particular mystery – that there wasn't one. I put the case of the captain who didn't disappear from my mind and got on with the research for the murder book. Yet every so often the case popped maddeningly back up again, and I wondered frequently about the real mystery: how did the story come about; was there a grain of truth behind the myth?

It was a year or so later, when scanning microfilm of the *Derbyshire Courier* for Saturday, August 8th 1846, that I came across the following macabre yet fascinating item which may provide the answer:

'Remarkable disappearance. – About forty years ago the father of Mr Thomas Dyson, cabinet maker, of Chesterfield, – whose death appeared in last week's Courier—resolved to settle himself and family in America, and proceeded to embark for that country, promising that, as soon as he had made suitable arrangements, he would immediately send for his wife and family. Years passed on, and nothing could be heard of him. However, some years ago, the remains of a skeleton were found concealed in a cleft of one of the rocks in the neighbourhood of Eyam, the skull of which was quite entire. Upon examining the skull there appeared certain irregularities in the formation of the teeth, from which it was conjectured to be that of old Mr Dyson. It is supposed that the old man was robbed and murdered, and the body afterwards conveyed to the cleft in the rock, in order to effect concealment. Mr Dyson had carried on the business of a carpet manufacturer at Chesterfield previous to his departure.'

What, I conjectured, if the 'Chesterfield lady' had been related to both Captain Wyatt and Thomas Dyson? What if she had collected much of the old family history, and had received in the process a garbled version of the relative who disappeared and the captain whose life was threatened yet continued to go out in the dark of night to observe the stars? The two events, passed down orally for several generations, coupled, maybe, with the story of how Wyatt had gone 'on the run' for six months while waiting for his trial to come to court, could have been so changed and conjoined that it is quite feasible that we finish up with the myth of the disappearing captain!

Clearly, there can be no way of knowing for certain, as Clarence Daniel and, almost certainly, his correspondent too, are dead, and their documents on the family history are not available to us. Yet for the researcher of myths the tale of the vanishing man who didn't serves to teach us two lessons: the first, always check your myth against known, verifiable historical facts, and second, that when you strip a myth down to what is known, the facts you reveal may often be more interesting than the fiction which has obscured them for so many years.

BIBLIOGRAPHY

A Guide to Eyam, by Clarence Daniel (the author, Edge View, Eyam; 1947), p.11.

The History of Magpie Mine, Sheldon, Derbyshire, by Lynn Willies, V S Roche, Noel Worley and T D Ford (Peak District Mines Historical Society, Mining Museum, Matlock Bath, Derbyshire; 1980).

'The Barker Family and Wyatt Lead Mining Businesses – 1730-1875', in *Bulletin of the Peak District Mines Historical Society*, **8,** No.6, Winter 1983 (Peak District Mines Historical Society, Mining Museum, Matlock Bath, Derbyshire).

'Delf View', by Clarence Daniel, in *Derbyshire Countryside*, **22,** No.2, February-March 1957, pp.22-23.

The Derbyshire Courier, Saturday, March 29th 1834, p.4, col.2.

The Derbyshire Times, Saturday, October 9th 1858, p.3, col.4.

The Derbyshire Courier, Saturday, August 8th 1846, p.2, col.7.

CHAPTER 3

Some Moot Aspects
of The Plague of Eyam
1665 – 1666

by Brian Robinson and Peter Gilbert

William Wood (1804-1865) (from *The Reliquary*, 1866). The cottage in which he lived is in the Lydgate, Eyam.

WILLIAM WOOD WAS A SELF-TAUGHT AND LIFE-long resident of Eyam, born in the village on 6 December 1804. He became a tax inspector, acted as assistant overseer of the poor and was librarian to the Mechanics' Institute in the village. His local claim to fame, however, derives from his book *The History and Antiquities of Eyam*, first published in 1842. This book is concerned largely with an outbreak of plague that occurred in the village during 1665 and persisted for just over a year. Unfortunately, Wood's writing style is somewhat over-allegorical, being couched in the most florid language with both the amorous and moral over-tones that so appealed to the Victorians. Indeed, parts of his account are more like a romantic novel than a history, for he re-counts thoughts and conversations of which he can have had no knowledge, even from tradition. Moreover, he fails to give adequate references to his documentary sources (mainly the entries in the parish register – probably the transcript (*vide in-fra*)) that supplemented the oral tradition. There is no doubt that Wood would have benefitted from the type of formal education that was so often wasted on those from more wealthy backgrounds for, by his own admission, his book was a 'rather hastily written work' by a man of an 'inappropriate situation in life for the attaining of philological perfection'. Nevertheless, his work surpassed all previously published studies of the Plague of Eyam and it ran into eight editions, the last appearing in 1903. Furthermore, even with all its imperfections it has until recently been the major source for the narrative of this disaster which befell Eyam and which over the past two and a half centuries has prompted the production of a plethora of fiction, drama, poetry and antiquarian writing. Such works cover the whole range of quality – many being indifferent by any criterion – and few add anything substantial to the story as related by Wood.

As the mass of secondary works of all kinds has steadily increased over the years, the truth about the Plague of Eyam has inevitably become encrusted by a rare mixture of fact and fiction, providing the deeply-rooted traditional tale which proves a strong tourist attraction. The tale relates how, on or about 2 September 1665, George Viccars, an itinerant tailor then lodging with the Cooper family in the village, received a box of textiles from London. Upon arrival, the contents of the box were found to be damp and so Viccars laid them out before the fire to dry off. Within a few hours he began to feel ill, on the next day had grown noticeably worse and on 6 September he died and was buried the following day, the first victim of the Plague of Eyam. The interpretation of this sequence of events is

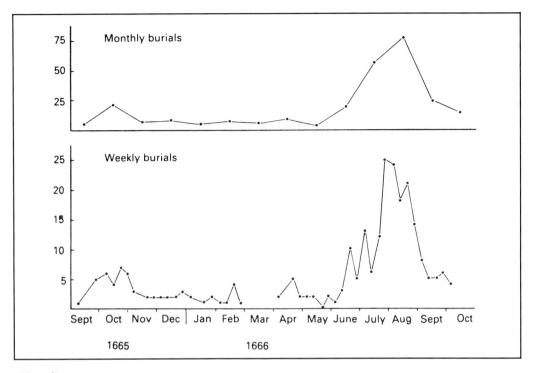

Figure 1. Mortality of the inhabitants of the village of Eyam in the Peak District of Derbyshire: September 1665 to October 1666 (from Twigg, p.193).

that the materials in the box harboured rat fleas which were carrying the bacterium of the bubonic plague, which at that time was raging in London.

Thus began the pestilence which, allegedly spread by the black rat, *Rattus rattus*, struck this Derbyshire village. The next victim, on 22 September 1665, was Edward Cooper, and within a few more days four of the Coopers' various near neighbours were likewise dead. October 1665 witnessed the death of 23 further victims, but then, with the approach of winter – said to have been a severe one – the spread of the disease was checked for some seven months (Figure 1).

However, June 1666 saw its return with a vengeance – 19 deaths. It was at this juncture that the villagers, led, in the absence of the squire and the wealthier residents who had already fled, by their young rector of only three years' standing in the community, William Mompesson (see Note 1), and by their former Puritan minister, Thomas Stanley (see Note 2), took three important decisions. As a result, there were no more organised funerals and churchyard burials – families buried their own dead in gardens or fields; the church was locked until the epidemic had passed and services were held in the open air – in a nearby natural amphitheatre known as Cucklett Delph; and, to prevent the spread of the disease beyond the parish, a cordon sanitaire was established around it. Although the village was to some extent self-sufficient, certain points on this boundary were designated at which necessary supplies from outside could be left, locations usually identified by stone troughs in which the money paid for the supplies could be left submerged in a mixture of vinegar and water, in the belief that this would disinfect the coins. In July 1666 the scourge raged even more fiercely – 57 deaths – and, during the following month, 79 people died, including Mompesson's wife, Katherine, on 25 August. Their children, George and Elizabeth, had been sent away earlier, as had some of the other children in the village, in the Mompessons' case to be cared for by relatives in Yorkshire. The last plague interment took place on 1 November 1666, by which time a total of 76 families had suffered some, or complete, bereavement and a total of 259 had died out of the village's population of about 350 (some claim the population to have been as low as 310).

Such is the traditionally accepted story of a tragedy filled with courage and self-sacrifice.

In recent years, however, attempts have been made to disentangle facts from the masses of legendary debris that, with the passage of time, have accumulated around them. The rose-tinted spectacles of sentiment and melodrama have been discarded, the short-comings of much of what is contained in the various accounts of the Eyam Plague have been recognised and Wood's honest but inadequate efforts of 1842 have been variously displaced in articles by Batho and Bradley and in passing by Twigg in his book (see bibliography below). The results of these scholarly re-appraisals of the Plague of Eyam, with particular reference to its aetiology, source, morbidity and associated incidence of mortality, and the village's quarantining, form the basis of the remainder of this chapter. In several instances, the conclusions are far from definite and, contrary to the impression left by the traditional tale, many facets of the Plague of Eyam remain puzzling and open to speculation.

The incidence of plague in Derbyshire

Outbreaks of plague outside large populous cities were not as rare as the nineteenth century writers imagined; indeed, Derbyshire was no stranger to plague before 1665. For example, from October 1586 to November 1587, Chesterfield, some twelve miles distant from Eyam, suffered what the parish register called 'The Great Plague of Chesterfield' that claimed between 275 and 290 lives in the town from a population of, probably, about 1,300. Whilst there were also a few victims in satellite hamlets, such as Calow, it seems likely that the town of Chesterfield itself bore practically the whole incidence. The mortality associated with the disease which struck Chesterfield was approximately that which befell the village of Eyam 79 years later and which killed approximately 245 victims from a population of between 850 and 1,000 (*vide infra*) during, very nearly, the same seasonal 13 months.

The pestilence also appeared just after the turn of the sixteenth century in Brimington (1603), Belper (1603, with 53 deaths), Ashbourne (1605, with 62 deaths) and Chesterfield again (1608 to 1609). The Darley Dale register for 1551 records that from 5th to 10th July were buried nine people who had died from 'ye sweatinge sicknesse'. The register at Hope records an outbreak of a highly contagious disease that killed a large number of children and others in the village in 1636. Serious outbreaks of plague occurred in the County Town itself in 1586, 1592, 1605 and 1636 (and, possibly, in 1665 which, if so, may have been the source of the disease that struck Eyam (*vide infra*)). In 1632 the hamlet of Curbar, within some three miles of Eyam, received a visitation that caused bereavement in several families. Unfortunately, this outbreak was not chronicled, but we are reminded of it by five slabs of roughly-hewn stone, inscribed with the initials T.C. 1632, A.C., O.C., N.C. and T.C., which lie in a group beside a public footpath below Curbar Edge. These are the grave-stones of Thomas and Ada Cundy and their children Olive, Nellie and young Thomas, who all lived near Curbar, in an isolated farm known as Grislow Field that was suddenly depopulated during the 1632 outbreak – no-one knows who buried the Cundys.

Thus, the disaster that struck Eyam during 1665 and 1666 was only the last of a series of similar tragedies that had occurred in other parts of the county over the previous eighty years. Eyam's case, however, appears to have caught the public's imagination, perhaps because it represents the final major incidence of plague, but more likely because of the cordon sanitaire which was thrown around the village, coupled with the many extant plague-related artefacts.

The aetiology of the disease that infected the people of Eyam
In early times, plague was a general name applied to diseases with high mortality occurring as an epidemic within a community. Included under this mantle were smallpox, cholera, typhoid, anthrax, bubonic plague, pneumonic plague and septicaemic plague.

The components usually accepted as being necessary for bubonic plague are rodents (often rats), fleas and the causative bacterium, *Yersinia pestis*. A convenient point to begin the plague cycle is with a carrier species of rodent such as the rat. The bacterium multiplies rapidly in the blood of this animal and produces an overwhelming septicaemia. If fleas are present on an infected rat, they will take a large number of bacteria, together with their blood meals, into their stomach. In about 12% of fleas, the bacteria become established in the stomach, dividing rapidly to form a solid mass that obstructs it. In this condition, further blood cannot enter the stomach. The flea consequently becomes very hungry and will feed on any warm-blooded animal it can find, including man. On such hosts, infected fleas will attempt to suck blood, causing the gullet to distend to its limit. Eventually, the elasticity of the gullet walls will cause it to contract and regurgitate blood back into the prey's wound. This blood has contacted and picked up the plague bacteria, which now enter the body of the second host. Furthermore, fleas defaecate as they feed, depositing faeces together with bacteria on to the skin. Scratching by the host to relieve the irritation caused by the flea bites rubs this material and the bacteria into the puncture made by the flea and also into other skin abrasions. Rats, and some other rodent species, can die from the septicaemia caused by bubonic plague bacteria. In such a situation, the fleas leave the body of the dead animal as it cools and seek an alternative host, preferably another rat, but, not being too particular, occasionally a human being, thus again establishing a route to human infection.

In humans, bubonic plague typically has an incubation period of two to eight days (dependent on the number of bacteria delivered by the flea at the time of feeding). During this period there is an increase in the numbers of bacterial cells in the bloodstream and in the associated lymph nodes which bind and immobilise foreign bodies that appear in the blood. The lymph nodes of the groin drain the legs and lower trunk, whereas those of the neck and armpits drain the upper body. Usually, white blood cells and immune responses in these nodes kill and digest invading organisms, thereby preventing their spread further in the body. If they fail to do this, and the plague bacteria are particularly resistant to such treatment, then the nodes shut off, preventing passage of contaminated blood and plasma to the rest of the body. An inflammatory reaction then ensues, causing the node to swell up. This, in association with continued growth of the organism, creates the buboes. Chemicals released by the 'frustrated' white blood cells (they are there but cannot do anything about the infection) cause massive host tissue damage at the lymph node, which further exacerbates the condition.

Thus bites on the legs and crotch lead to buboes of the groin, bites to the arms and neck to buboes of the neck and armpits, and bites to the trunk to buboes at nodes scattered throughout the gastrointestinal tract. In spite of these very obvious symptoms, it is important to realise that none of the lesions associated with bubonic plague is exclusive to this disease, not even the bubo itself, which may relate to any acute septicaemia.

Plague can also manifest itself in other ways. In typical bubonic plague, the disease is insidious in onset, but rapid in progress. Occasionally, though, the lymph nodes do not obstruct the passage of the organism and large numbers of bacteria thereby get into the bloodstream. The infection then besets the animal in a body-wide attack. In this situation, namely septicaemic plague, sudden death occurs generally within hours of the onset of symptoms, although this is still from two to eight days after infection. Cases of septicaemic plague are infrequent, but it is when this form of plague is in evidence that the human flea, *Pulex irritans*, may operate in spreading the disease. This flea can take in large numbers of bacteria and thereby carry the disease from man to man without the need of an intermediary rat to provide a fresh source of infection. In bubonic plague, even in fatal cases, the lymph nodes have prevented the spread of bacteria and they are few and far between in the blood. The human flea would therefore be ineffective as a man to man transmitter, since there would be insufficient bacteria to colonise the flea's stomach. Consequently, bubonic plague scarcely ever spreads from man to man, even when human fleas are plentiful.

During the course of bubonic plague, organisms may occasionally find their way into victims' lungs to produce a third variant of the disease, pneumonic plague, in which the bacteria are found in the bronchopneumonic areas of the body and are evident in the sputum. Pneumonic plague is highly infectious and may be readily transmitted from man to man as airborne droplets. Every time the victim coughs the bacteria are sprayed into the air to be breathed in by those nearby. Such inhalation of the plague bacterium initiates an infection in the lung that develops into pneumonic plague and is nearly always fatal (and very rapidly so). This enables the bacteria to spread without the intermediation of fleas. The outbreak at Eyam was, however, too geographically extended to have been caused by this form of plague.

Outbreaks of human bubonic plague have been accepted as occurring only under certain conditions. Firstly, there must be a large number of infected rats in close proximity to human beings, and, secondly, the infected rats must act as hosts to a type of flea that will feed readily on human blood. Bubonic plague spreads most actively among man and rats in those places and at those times where, or when, the density of a species of flea known as *Xenopsylla cheopis* is high. Furthermore, this species of flea prefers, as its host, the black rat, *Rattus rattus*, to the brown rat, *Rattus norvegicus*.

It has been claimed that the black rat would have been able to breed undisturbed, and to survive the winter of 1665-1666, in the timber-framed and thatched roofs of the houses in Eyam. However, as Professor J N Tarn, Roscoe Professor of Architecture in the University of Liverpool and an authority on the architecture of the Peak District, has pointed out (Bradley, pages 66 and 80), the majority of houses in Eyam at this date were 'likely to have been constructed of stone, with earth or stone floors and roofed with stone slabs', thus denying *Rattus rattus* its alleged abode. Furthermore, Dr Graham Twigg, Senior Lecturer in Zoology at the University of London and an authority on rats and rodent-borne diseases, is of the opinion (Twigg, page 192) that, in the bleak environment of Eyam, 'it is impossible to believe that *Rattus rattus* could have survived if introduced, let alone have formed a widespread population'. In a similar manner, the climatic conditions of this Peakland village, especially during the winter months, would not have been favourable to the flea *Xenopsylla cheopis*, which, as noted by Batho (page 84), requires a temperature of 65 to 76F and a relatively dry atmosphere for a maximum population density.

What disease, if not bubonic plague, might then have been responsible for the terrible carnage amongst the residents of Eyam in late 1665, and especially during the five months of June to October 1666?

The only contemporary descriptions of the symptoms of the disease that befell the inhabitants of Eyam, and even these are somewhat in the nature of passing comments, appear in two of the three letters written by William Mompesson during the pestilence. One of these, written on 31 August 1666 to his two children who had been sent away to safety a few months earlier to the Leekes at Barnburgh, near Doncaster, concerned the death of their mother from the sickness a week earlier. Referring to his attempts to treat his wife, Mompesson writes 'I gave her several sweating antidotes, which had no kind operation, but rather scalded and inflamed her more, whereupon her dear head was distempered, which put her upon many incoherencies'. Later, on 20 November 1666, in a letter to an uncle, John Beilby, in Yorkshire, he refers to the 'disfigured bodies' of what he took to be the last fourteen victims of the plague, and later in his text to the cure of his manservant: 'My man had the Distemper and upon the appearance of a Tumor I applied several Chymical Antidotes which had a very kind operation and with ye Blessing of God kept the venom from the Heart and after the rising broke, he was very well....'. This later statement probably refers to a bubo of sorts, but, as stated already, such swellings are not exclusive to bubonic plague. It is surprising also that if the disease had been bubonic plague Mompesson did not mention somewhere in at least one of his three letters the gross buboes that would have been very apparent on the majority of the victims.

Twigg (page 218) is of the opinion that 'anthrax would seem a more appropriate disease in the Peak village of Eyam than would bubonic plague'. However, this is unlikely since, were it to have been the case, there would have been expected an associated abnormal death rate amongst farm animals, which does not appear to have occurred in Eyam. Furthermore, in Africa, where anthrax is still endemic, its transfer to humans is minimal. On the other hand, Twigg argues quite rightly (pages 218-219) that since 'The people of the village were prevented or dissuaded from leaving the village, as a result of which the death rate was high' this may be 'evidence of a disease which was either contagious or infectious from person to person'. He furthermore appears to suggest (page 219) that typhoid may have been responsible, although the 'Tumor' described by Mompesson would appear to be at variance with this and the mortality was too high. Such factors are also incompatible with smallpox which, furthermore, had it been the causative disease, would surely have elicited comment from Mompesson regarding the scarring of survivors. On the other hand, although it too would be at apparent variance with the 'Tumor' referred to by Mompesson, perhaps the measles virus, which is known to have caused a 60% mortality when introduced into isolated Indian communities, was the organism responsible for the plague in Eyam.

Although from argument presented in this and the following section it may be claimed with some degree of confidence that bubonic plague was not the disease responsible for the Plague of Eyam, the aetiology for the catastrophe that befell the village is far from established. It could, nevertheless, be established from a pathological investigation of the remains of victims, involving a search for bacterial and viral DNA. The chances of success for such a study from skeletal remains alone may be low, but, since bone has a vascular system, they should not be

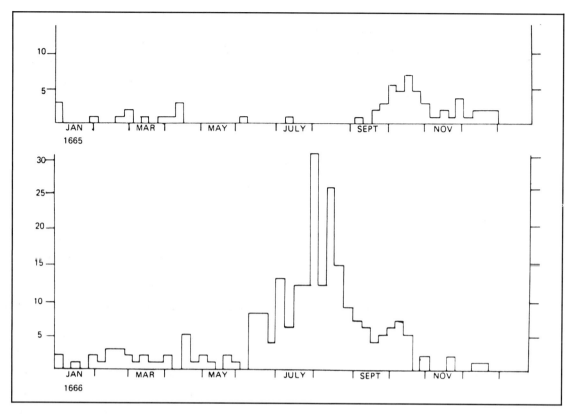

Figure 2. Weekly totals of burials in Eyam during 1665 and 1666 (from Bradley, p.87).

ignored. Soft tissue specimens, such as might survive in a lead coffin, would most likely be required, but whether such luxuries would have been afforded the dead of Eyam – even the rector's wife – during this period is very doubtful. Moreover, the bodies were almost certainly limed upon burial, which would certainly obviate the survival of post-mortem soft tissue and possibly even that of the necessary genetic residues that may have been in the bones.

One plague or two?

The possibility that the residents of Eyam suffered from two sequential epidemics, one from September to November 1665 and another from June to October 1666 has been suggested by Bradley (pages 70-71) from a consideration of the chronological record of deaths (Figure 1; see also Figure 2). The total number of burials from November 1665 to May 1666 inclusive was 47. Since the previous highest total for the same period was 26 (in 1639-1940 and 1650-1651) (although in none of these seven months considered separately is the mortality much higher than other peaks during the seventeenth century), Bradley at one point suggested that 'All this makes it appear that some epidemic was in progress throughout the winter, and the fact that no previous winter had produced mortality on this scale appears to lend some support to the suggestion that the plague epidemic of September and October continued on a smaller scale throughout the winter and recrudesced in June 1666'. On the other hand, J F D Shrewsbury in his book *A History of Bubonic Plague in the British Isles* (Cambridge University Press, 1970) asserts categorically that human plague can persist only through exceptionally mild winters [not the sort expected at Eyam], though it may persist amongst the rat population and reappear as a human disease when the warm weather returns; although at this juncture it should be borne in mind that it is by no means certain – in fact it is more than unlikely – that the disease which ravaged the residents of Eyam was bubonic plague. In fact, when the 47 deaths are examined in greater detail there is, according to Bradley (page 71), no clear evidence for the persistence of a plague in Eyam during the winter months.

Three victims in one family occurred in early November and were very possibly the last victims of the 1665 plague outbreak. A further 18 deaths were spread amongst 17 families and therefore give no sign of the infection being passed on inside the family. One death was within the Hawkesworth family, but is excluded because it is confused by two, or possibly three, families being entangled. This leaves the following six families, showing the surname and burial dates of its deceased members, for further consideration:

Rowland: 5 November, 1 December, 15 January, 14 February
Rowbotham: 9 December, 24 December, 1 January (2 deaths)
Rowe: 14 December, 15 December, 19 December
Blackwall: 24 December, 21 February, 2 March, 6 April, 16 April
Wilson: 22 December, 28 January, 15 February, 17 February, 18 February, 1 March
Thorpe: 15 April, 30 April (2 deaths)

Bradley asserts (page 71) that of these records, only three, namely Rowbotham, Rowe and Thorpe, display the intra-familial plague pattern, with the Thorpes being possibly the first victims of the 1666 outbreak. The intervals between burials in the other families are longer than one would expect in the same family if all were caused by plague. Indeed, pneumonic plague is so virulent that it would take a whole family almost together. Bradley quite rightly concludes (page 79) that 'In Eyam, the occurrence of unusually high winter mortality without any clear sign of a plague pattern within the affected families leaves the issue [as to whether or not the plague persisted in the village throughout the winter of 1665-1666] in doubt'. Unfortunately, no records are extant relating to the number who were infected but survived, for with such information it is possible to estimate an infection's mortality, namely the number of deaths in proportion to the number of those infected. Such data might distinguish not only the 1665 and 1666 Eyam outbreaks from each other, but also distinguish them from the well-established mortality of bubonic plague.

The source of the plague at Eyam
In his treatise *A discourse on the Plague*, first published in 1720 under the title *A short discourse concerning pestilential contagion, and the methods to be used to prevent it*, Richard Mead writes with reference to the Eyam plague that 'The plague was likewise at Eham in the Peak of Derbyshire, being brought thither by means of a Box sent from London [where the Great Plague was then raging] to a Taylor in that village, containing some Materials relating to his Trade . . . A Servant, who opened the foresaid Box, complaining that the Goods were damp, was ordered to dry them at the Fire; but in so doing it was seized with the Plague and died . . .'. Although Mead's work, the first printed discussion of the plague in Eyam, did not appear until 1720, over half a century after the event, his authority was George Mompesson, the son of the then late William Mompesson. The credibility of the account is nevertheless open to doubt, since, as pointed out by John G Clifford in 1989, the first victim of the plague was George Viccars, a travelling tailor who was lodging with Mary Cooper, the widow of a lead miner, and her two young sons. Furthermore, there was little likelihood of a lead miner's widow being in a position to have servants. Clearly, George Mompesson's memory was at fault, understandably so since he was only four years old at the time of the Plague of Eyam.

It would appear that this account of the arrival of the plague in the village was accepted and elaborated upon by Wood in 1842 (page 42) when he wrote 'It is, however, matter of fact, that this terrible plague was brought from London to Eyam in a box of old clothes and some tailor's patterns of cloth' and went on to describe how the box had arrived in Eyam on 2 or 3 September 1665, when it was unpacked and the damp clothes had been hung out to dry by Viccars, who had then been seized with violent sickness and other symptoms, grown horribly worse on the second day, being delirious and with large swellings on his neck and groin, shown the plague spot on his breast

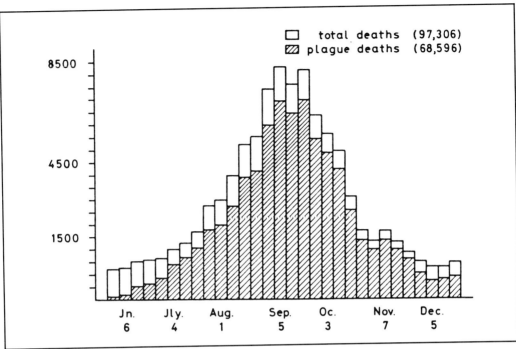

8500

4500

1500

total deaths (97,306)
plague deaths (68,596)

| Jn. | Jly. | Aug. | Sep. | Oc. | Nov. | Dec. |
| 6 | 4 | 1 | 5 | 3 | 7 | 5 |

Figure 3. Total deaths and plague deaths in London, 1665 (from Twigg, p.194).

on the third day, and died on 6 September. Although Bradley points out (page 64) that by the eighth edition of Wood's book – in 1903 – this account of the plague's first appearance in Eyam was qualified by the caveats 'most positively stated' and 'according to traditional accounts', it had by then become widely accepted as fact rather than possibility.

Wood's account raises considerable difficulty in that a significant feature is the rapidity of the disease's onset. This is characteristic of both pneumonic and septicaemic plagues, but these are both eliminated from consideration since the next victim did not die until a fortnight later. An alternative possibility, a severe attack of bubonic plague, would be eliminated by the very short incubation period, only a few hours, which would also eliminate other possibilities such as smallpox, typhoid and anthrax, notwithstanding that inhalation of anthrax spores in large numbers – but far in excess of those that would be expected to be carried in cloth – will cause asphyxia and death very rapidly. Alternatively, although Viccars may indeed have become ill soon after opening a box of clothes received from London, we have no verification that he contracted his illness *from* the clothes and he may have already been incubating the disease, whatever it may have been, when he opened the box. In fact, it is significant that Viccars was an *itinerant* tailor, and he may well have contracted his illness during the course of his journeying. The box of textiles – if it existed at all – and its opening were very likely purely coincidental, despite the opinion of Batho (page 86) who concludes, for a reason difficult to understand, that 'the traditional explanation of the coming of the plague to Eyam is, however, the more probable'.

Furthermore, that the disease responsible for the plague in Eyam during 1666 was different from that which raged in London in 1665 is suggested from a consideration of the relative movements in the totals of deaths, as measured by the burials, from these two epidemics (Figures 2 and 3). In Eyam, the peak of the epidemic was reached during the last week in July and the first week in August, whereas in London the death rate maximised in the three weeks beginning 5 September. This, in the warmer environment of the city of London, where there is little doubt that the disease was bubonic plague, was a month later than in the cooler climate of the Pennine village, whereas if the two diseases had been the same, the converse might have been expected, assuming that there were no dramatic climatic differences between the summer months of 1665 and 1666. In addition, in London, plague deaths rose from a very low level at the end of May and reached an epidemic peak three months later, whereas in Eyam, with a much more scattered population, the peak was reached after a significantly shorter period, namely seven weeks after the low period of the first week in June. Once again, had the two diseases been the same the converse might have been expected, notwithstanding the confinement of the villagers in June 1666 (*vide infra*).

A further possible source of the pestilence that struck Eyam at the beginning of September 1665 was the plague that, according to Hutton, was severely affecting Derby in that year. According to Wood, Eyam Wakes took place on Sunday, 20 August, in 1665, namely 13 or 14 days before Viccars fell ill and 17 days before he died. If a rat flea brought to the Wakes were the source of infection, this would fit nicely into the period between these festivities and Viccars' death. The interval would be in accord with the incubation period of bubonic plague or of other possible diseases. If, on the other hand, a human flea was responsible for the transmission of bubonic plague directly from a visitor to Viccars, rather than by a host rat, the incubation period would be expected to be much shorter. More seriously, whether or not there was a plague in Derby during 1665 is uncertain, since an examination reported by Bradley (page 69) of the registers of the Derby parishes for that year revealed no excessive mortality, namely nothing that could suggest an epidemic outbreak.

So not only the aetiology of the disease responsible for the

Plague of Eyam, but also how it came to the village remains in doubt and open to speculation.

The death rate from the Plague of Eyam

The parish of Eyam comprises some 3,000 acres; the main settlement is the village of Eyam, with smaller settlements at Foolow and Grindleford Bridge, some 2 and 1 miles respectively in opposite directions from Eyam village, together with a number of small groups of farmhouses and isolated farms.

In 1842, Wood (pages 56 and 79) suggested that at the onset of the plague the population of Eyam was about 350, 'or perhaps a few more'. However, that there was some confusion by Wood between the parish and the village was recognised in 1964 by Batho, who made a study of the Compton Census. This is an ecclesiastical return made in 1676 in which the incumbent was required, in effect, to state the number of persons in the parish who were of communicant age. Batho deduced that the population of the village ten years after the plague was about 750. This, considering further that the wealthier inhabitants at the west end of the village are known to have mostly fled in the spring of 1666 and that a proportion of Eyam's population consisted of seasonal workers in lead mines, led him to conclude that 'On any reckoning, it seems improbable that the village could have been depopulated to the degree which has been commonly suggested'. Thirteen years later, Bradley (page 67) reported an extension of Batho's population studies in which not only the 1676 Compton Census but the parish registers – making assumptions about the birth and death rates prevailing at the appropriate period – were examined. These studies show that at the onset of the plague, Eyam parish contained at least 246 families, from which it was reasonable to conclude that the population was unlikely to have been less than 850, and might well have been 1,000 or even more.

Furthermore, it is not clear exactly how many of the residents of the parish of Eyam died of the plague. In the letter concerning the plague that William Mompesson wrote on 20 November 1666 to his uncle, John Beilby, in Yorkshire, the rector stated that 'Here hath been 76 Families visited within my Parish, out of which have died 259. Blessed be God, all our fears are over, for none have died here of the infection since the Eleventh of October,...'. Wood, however, taking the burial of Joseph Mortin, on 14 October 1666 as noted by Bradley (page 72), as the final one due to the plague, counts a total of 267 burials and ascribes the difference between this and Mompesson's to the possibility that the rector disregarded deaths which he knew were not caused by the plague. Unfortunately, Wood's list of victims is incomplete, for he omits the names of Edyna Mower, John Thornley and Thomas Hawksworth which appear in the transcript of the parish register (*vide infra*) – one of the primary data sources available to him – as plague victims number 69, 76 and 154 respectively, who were buried on 15 June, 18 June and 4 August 1666 respectively. Interestingly, the same omissions, and other errors, namely involving spelling, that appear in Wood's compilation, also appear in the list of plague victims published, over several editions, nearly a century later by another local writer, Clarence Daniel, clearly indicating that he had simply copied Wood's efforts rather than consulting the available primary source. This register numbers all the plague deaths sequentially and indicates that the last such death, the 260th, occurred on 1 November 1666. These numbered entries are contained in a document that is itself a transcription of the original registers from 1630 to 1705, reputedly made by a later rector, Joseph Hunt. Comparison by Bradley (page 82) of this transcription with the copies of the original register that were sent to the Registry of the Diocese of Lichfield – of which Eyam was then a component – at intervals of roughly three years, over the years from 1660 to 1667, show significant differences. Thus, the register for 1665 contains 107 entries; there are three entries in the register but not in the transcript and four in the transcript but not in the register, with four serious discrepancies between the register and the transcript. For the 1666 register and transcript, the corresponding entries and error counts are 279, 6, 0 and 5.

As well as these differences, 16 names in the register for the period concerned have been omitted from the numbered transcript, presumably deaths from causes other than the plague, and, despite the Rector's assertion, the final nine burials took place between 12 October and 1 November. Whilst the discrepancy between these nine burials and Mompesson's observations remains unresolved, it is certain that during the plague period other diseases, such as infant deaths and respiratory diseases amongst the elderly during the winter months, would have continued to take their toll. Indeed, Bradley shows (pages 74, 89 and 90) that 'over the three decades prior to the plague, burial averages fluctuated between twenty and twenty-six per annum and were slightly higher in the two decades following the plague'. This suggests that not 16, as indicated from the transcript of the parish register, but in the region of 25 deaths from causes other than plague would have occurred over the plague period. If this were to have been so, then the number of deaths from the plague would have been 243 or thereabouts, and, being from a population of between 850 and 1,000, this gives a mortality associated with the Plague of Eyam of approximately the same dimensions as that of the Plague of Chesterfield in 1586-1587 (*vide supra*).

Consideration of these above data shows that between a quarter and a third of the population of the parish Eyam died of the plague. This a far cry from the five-sixths as claimed by Wood (page 40), erroneously comparing the total number of deaths in the parish with the population of only the village, or, at the most, the central township. Even such an otherwise accomplished author as F Wolverson Cope (1976) states that 'At that time the population of Eyam was about 350 and of these all but fifty died in the course of seven [sic] months' – such is the stuff of legend! Indeed, Bradley further shows (pages 76-77) that the township itself lost no more than a half of its original population, and probably less, which, he notes, comes near to the sort of death rate quoted by modern authorities for plague epidemics and is in accord with the account of T Short, who, in his *A General Chronological History of the Air*, published in 1749 (pages 339-340), writes, in relation to plague, 'As to Eyam in

Figure 4. Bradshaw Hall, Eyam (circa 1860) (from the *Journal of the Derbyshire Archaeological and Natural History Society*, 1884, **6**, p.126), viewed looking northward toward its front. The ruins of this building are still a prominent feature in the village, despite the fact that in September 1961 the southwest corner of its main front collapsed and, in the following January, after gales, the greater part of the remainder of the building fell to the ground.

Derbyshire, here it quickly killed between 2 and 300, or near half the People of the Village'.

The quarantining of Eyam in 1666

More than any other aspect of the Plague of Eyam, the famous cordon sanitaire that was established around the village in June 1666 appears to have caught the public imagination and to have consequently been subjected to sentimental distortion. Thus its objective re-appraisal by Batho in 1964 (pages 88-90) was long overdue.

In 1565, Francis Bradshaw married Ann Stafford of Eyam, who inherited considerable estate in the village and its neighbourhood, including Stafford Hall which had been built during the reign of Henry VI. It was their great-grandson, also called Francis, who commenced the building of an extension at the eastern end of Stafford Hall, to be known as Bradshaw Hall, and which, now in ruins, is known as Eyam 'Old Hall' (Figure 4).

However, the extension was never completed since, when the plague broke out in Eyam in the autumn of 1665, the Bradshaws fled to Brampton in Yorkshire, and never returned to the village (see Note 3). Indeed, by April 1666, most of the wealthier inhabitants, at the west end of the village, had left, an exodus that also included George and Elizabeth Mompesson, the two children of the rector. All these departures were some weeks before the remainder of the inhabitants, the poorer elements, were confined behind the famous cordon sanitaire in June 1666, with the co-operation of the local aristocracy and clergy outside Eyam as well as the leadership from within the parish, namely by the rector and Thomas Stanley. This cordon sanitaire has been discussed in some detail by Batho (pages 89, 90) and Bradley (page 79).

Contrary to myth and hype, heroism does not appear to have been the motivation behind this confinement. Most of the remaining villagers would have been too poor to abandon their livelihoods or to have had anywhere to escape to, and, in any case, by then 'owing to the terror which the very name of their village caused in all the country around', they would have found it difficult, if not impossible, to leave.

The sacrifice, if sacrifice it were, was, as modern medical knowledge has demonstrated, misguided, and what would otherwise have been a rural outbreak of disease with a fairly low death rate was provided with conditions more akin to those of a severe urban epidemic, with an associated high rate of morbidity. Flight would have been, without doubt, the better course of action in the spring of 1666. Instead, 'shut up in their narrow valley, the villagers perished helplessly like a stricken flock of sheep'. This quarantining of the villagers of Eyam during the summer of 1666 was certainly a grim mistake – and the Plague of Eyam was a disaster that need not have happened - but it may be excusable if it was effected in accord with the knowledge and practice of the times, times when medical 'science' had progressed no further than, for example, relying upon the monarch's touch as a cure for scrofula, a tubercular infection of the lymph nodes. Mompesson and Stanley were, without doubt, prompted by a genuine concern for the safety of the people outside Eyam and acted according to contemporary knowledge, and are therefore to be commended for their courage and not condemned for their lack of modern understanding.

Post-plague recovery and myth
There is no doubt that the epidemic that struck the parish of Eyam had traumatic effects. However, although the suffering of the people of Eyam was added to by their enforced isolation (sacrifice or sacrificed?), the mortality at Eyam was not significantly different from those caused by epidemics elsewhere. Bradley (pages 75 and 92) shows that of the 246 families whose existence during or immediately before the plague can be established, 157 (nearly 64%) escaped the plague; of the 89 families which suffered plague-period burials only 17 became extinct, and 172 families are known or are likely to have remained in existence after the plague, namely some 70% of those existing immediately before the plague. These data and that from sources including baptisms and marriages in the parish in the years immediately before, during and immediately after the plague, do not give the impression of a 'devastated' parish as suggested by the traditional tale. Recovery of the community was, in fact, quite rapid, and Bradley (page 75) asserts that 'The evidence suggests, then, that the effects of the plague on the parish as a whole were not so disastrous as to prevent it from re-establishing itself demographically in quite a short time and without heavy immigration of families from outside'.

Thomas Stanley died in Eyam in August 1670 and was buried there – sadly his grave is unmarked. By this time Mompesson had also left the village – he became rector of Eakring in Nottinghamshire in 1670, again under Savile's ever-obliging patronage, and subsequently a prebendary of Southwell. Oral tradition has it that he was dogged for some years by superstition about the plague and that, upon his appointment to Eakring, 'he humoured the apprehensive people by living in a hut in Rufford Park until they were satisfied that he was immune from infection'. Local legend and hype would also have it that he was refused the pulpit at Eakring church and preached beneath an ash tree until the fears of his new parishioners were dispelled. The tree, known as the 'Pulpit Ash', is to this day commemorated by a stone erected on the site in 1893 after it had been blown down in a gale. However, to offer a more convincing explanation for Mompesson's preaching in the open air at Eakring, Batho (page 91) quotes the following letter, dated 11 May 1672, from the rector to his patron – by this time Lord Savile – from which it seems likely that the village church was ruinous and perhaps unsafe to use (as were many such churches following neglect or vandalism during the period of the Commonwealth between 1649 and 1660):

> 'My Lord
> I am desired by my parishioners of Eakring to request your charitable assistance towards the rebuilding of their Church, which must be pulled downe to the very foundacion, & the timber is so miserably ruinous that nothing thereof will serve in its place agayne; to make all good is the desire but above the capacity of the people. If something be not speedily done, all our lyves will be exposed to danger & it's impossible for soe small & poore a parish to create such a structure, & your lordship's charity herein will buy an eternal bond from us all. My Lord Dorchester has given twenty pounds & if we could raise 40 li. more in contribution, I question not but we could complete the worke.'

Batho also reports that an inspection of Eakring Church reveals that a major reconstruction occurred in the 1670s, concluding that 'Oral tradition is a capricious recorder'.

Clarence Daniel was, like William Wood before him, a local author born and bred and, in his book upon Eyam, which ran through many editions, he used uncritically almost the whole of Wood's story of the plague and introduced into it yet further thoughts and conversations that would be incapable of substantiation. Furthermore, he quotes the so-called 'plague register' verbatim from Wood's book and, in doing so, inevitably reproduces the many errors (vide supra) introduced into the list by the earlier writer, an unfortunate propagation that could have been avoided if he had used the primary local source available to him, the Hunt transcription of the parish registers.

Daniel is, furthermore, unwilling to accept even Batho's reasonable explanation of Mompesson's open-air preaching at

Eakring, stating that his 'argument has little validity; its three main weaknesses being that (1) it is scarcely feasible the congregation would be expected to walk nearly half a mile out of the village for temporary services which (2) would hardly have been held in the open because of possible inclement weather, and (3) a subsequent patron of the living would never have gone to the expense of erecting a memorial to mark the temporary closure of the church'.

Not only is oral tradition a capricious recorder. In common with local hype, it is loath to die!

Note 1: Under the patronage of Sir George Savile of Rufford, Mompesson had previously been the Vicar of Scalby, near his native Seamer (near Scarborough) for a short time, and also of Wellow – both in 1662. However, later in the same year Savile appointed him to Eyam, a far more important living.

Note 2: Though removed from office in 1660 at the Restoration, Stanley was still held in high regard by many of the villagers.

Note 3: Given the circumstances of their departure, they could hardly return. This left a vacancy for a village squire figure in the then prevailing feudal society (today there are still those who expect to be fawned to and, even more pathetic, those – especially in rural areas – who are content to be fawners). This vacancy would appear to have been opportunely filled, but not until some years after the plague all clear, by a branch of a family by the name of Wright, from the nearby village of Great Longstone, who had, in pre-plague times, purchased estates in Eyam, where their descendants can still be found.

BIBLIOGRAPHY

Batho, G R, 'The plague of Eyam: A tercentenary re-evaluation', in *Derbyshire Archaeological Journal*, 1964, **84**, pp.81-91.

Bradley, Leslie, 'The most famous of all English plagues. A detailed analysis of the plague at Eyam, 1665-6' in *The plague reconsidered. A new look at its origins and effects in 16th and 17th century England* (A local population studies supplement, 1977), pp.63-94.

Clifford, John G, *Eyam Plague, 1665-1666* (the author, Eyam; 1989).

Cope, F Wolverson, *Geology explained in the Peak District* (David and Charles, Newton Abbot and London; 1976), p.101.

Daniel, Clarence, *The story of Eyam plague, with a guide to the village* (Bakewell and Wye Valley Press; 1991), and earlier editions.

Furness, Peter, 'Memoir of the late William Wood, of Eyam', in *The Reliquary*, 1866, pp.121-131.

Godfrey, W E, 'The plague of Chesterfield, 1586-7', in *Journal of the Derbyshire Archaeological and Natural History Society*, 1954, **74**, pp.32-42.

Hutton, W, *The History of Derby* (Nichols, Son, and Bentley, London; 1817), pp.194-5.

Mead, Richard, *A discourse on the plague* (1744 – the ninth edition): the section of this publication (pp.149-151) appertaining to the Plague of Eyam is reproduced by Bradley (p.80).

Reports on the condition of Bradshaw Hall, Eyam, in *Derbyshire Archaeological Journal*, 1961, **81**, p.151; 1962, **82**, p.11.

Short, T, *A general chronological history of the air* (1749), vol.i: the section of this publication (pp.339-340) appertaining to the Plague of Eyam is reproduced by Bradley (p.80).

Twigg, Graham, *The Black Death: a biological reappraisal* (Batsford Academic and Educational, London; 1984), in particular pp.192-5, 218-9.

Wood, William, *The history and antiquities of Eyam; with a full and particular account of the great plague which desolated that village, A.D.1666* (Miller, Newgate Street; Whitaker, Sheffield; Atkinson, Chesterfield; Goodwin, Bakewell; and the author, Eyam; 1842).

CHAPTER 4

Give a Man a Good Name

by Julie Bunting

William Newton
(1750-1830).
From a drawing by
Sir Francis
Chantrey, R.A.

IT IS A SHAMEFUL FACT THAT MILLS THROUGHOUT
England contributed to the Industrial Revolution largely
through the exploitation of destitute orphans, held in virtual
bondage to their masters.

The cruel treatment of children in the mills was exposed in

1832 with the publication of *A Memoir of Robert Blincoe*. In his childhood Blincoe had suffered a woeful apprenticeship at Litton Mill on the River Wye under the notoriously cruel Ellis Needham and his sons.

Yet only a few miles downstream from Litton stood Cressbrook Mill, long held in high regard for the exemplary treatment of its apprentices by their master, William Newton.

Born at Abney in 1750, William Newton grew up to become a carpenter. He also pursued the gentle musings of a poet and from 1783 his very fair attempts were encouraged by Miss Anna Seward, daughter of a former rector of Eyam and a poet herself. But Newton still had to earn a living and his skills as a framesmith led him into the cotton spinning industry. In 1786 Anna Seward advanced him a generous loan enabling him to buy a third partnership in a mill, almost certainly Litton. She would later claim, as confirmation of her own perceptive judgement, that within five years of being a £50-a-year carpenter Newton had made his first £1,000.

Around 1797 Newton withdrew from the mill partnership, only to suffer bankruptcy before finding work in Cheshire. Shortly after Anna Seward's death in 1809 his fortunes improved considerably with his appointment as manager of Cressbrook Mill. A factory inspector's report of 1811 noted that Cressbrook Mill was 'clean' and there is little doubt that this observation extended to the food. The apprentices were working from 6.00am to 8.00pm with an hour for dinner – hours which raised no eyebrows in those days and compared most favourably with those imposed at Litton Mill.

William Newton continued to preside at Cressbrook without ever apparently incurring official censure, although few references to the mill survive before the publication of *Vignettes of Derbyshire* in 1824. Author Mary Sterndale is believed to have visited Newton during the previous year.

It was this visit which resulted in the highly complimentary, oft-quoted reference to 'this illumined palace raised by the power of magic'. From the lengthy description in her book it seems that Mary Sterndale spent many hours at 'this fine establishment, this glory of a commercial nation' without finding one bad word to say.

She was pleased to confirm that the utmost decorum was upheld between boys and girls, each one of whom enjoyed a good night's sleep in a comfortable bed. There is further praise for the scrupulous attention given to personal cleanliness. Readers were especially uplifted to learn how the boys were taught 'The Heavenly Science' of music, with the girls in their separate room participating in the harmony so that 'The hallelujahs of Handel fill the valley'. It was pleasant, too, to picture the pretty scene of happy girls sewing for pleasure as they sat beside the river, or wandering at will in the dale when work was done.

Mary Sterndale entertained hopes that the young internees might become 'humanized' under the influence of the building which housed them, an edifice which inspired her to compare its soft indoor light with 'the dim religious light of monastic cloisters'. Nevertheless, she approved the enforcement of constant and regular industry and made no quarrel with the hours of work.

The operations of Newton received further praise in the contemporary account of a man with whom he fell into conversation whilst out walking. The stranger was welcomed into the Newton household, where he made a sketch of its master. This artist was Derbyshire-born Francis Chantrey.

By now Newton had handed over some of the day-to-day work at the mill to his son, Henry. William Newton died just before his 80th birthday in 1830 and was buried in Tideswell churchyard. A glowing obituary was composed by Mary Sterndale.

Two years later the Peak District's culpable role in the factory system was exposed to public outrage in Blincoe's damning pamphlet, yet it contained nothing to mar the fine reputation of William Newton. In 1849, however, first-hand accounts of two more former parish apprentices were published in *The Ashton Chronicle* and these contained harrowing claims about Cressbrook Mill (republished in *The Dark Satanic Mills*, 1980, edited by Edmund and Ruth Frow). Whilst the editor of this publication was a Chartist clergyman who compared the English factory system with slavery, he confined himself to testifying as to the truthfulness of the writers, leaving them to tell their stories in their own words.

The accounts are anonymous, except that in the first the author is addressed just once as John and he recalls his apprentice number at Cressbrook Mill as 253, with which all his clothes were numbered. Born in Bethnal Green in 1805 and orphaned by the age of six, his first apprenticeship was at Litton Mill, an even worse ordeal than his second – at Cressbrook, where he spent over three years from about 1819. The second memoir tells of working life at Cressbrook Mill as experienced by a woman who at the age of ten had become a bound apprentice there.

That both writers really had worked at the mill is clear from their familiarity with its buildings, hidden from outside eyes behind a high wall set with heavy gates. There is mention too of Bury-me-Wick: two rows of paid workers' houses in a spot which to this day is known by that name only to locals.

Added credibility comes from the naming of people who came into contact with the apprentices, like the Taddington overseer named Mycott but known as the Old Sergeant. He once instructed Newton to reclothe the little group of ragged boys who had walked barefoot over snow-covered hills from Cressbrook to ask him for official help. Others are mentioned by name: Messrs Knowles the Litton tailors, father and son, and factory watchmen Hancock and Brown. A master carder called Thomas Birks was known to the children as Tom-the-Devil for his persistent cruelty, almost equalled by his stand-in, William Hughes. An overlooker named James Birch is remembered for beating one Sarah Goodling to the floor three times, only hours before she was found dead.

Master over this vicious little world was William Newton, unrecognisable in the apprentices' memoirs from the fatherly figure known to Mary Sterndale. And Mrs Helen Newton, who shared in the management of the apprentices, could allegedly show a very different face to that of the 'domestic deity' who so favourably impressed the same visitor.

In her recollections, the former girl apprentice told how her elder brother was already at Cressbrook when she was taken there to see him at the age of ten by her widowed mother. Mrs Newton gave them such a warm welcome that the woman not only disregarded complaints from her son about his treatment but was persuaded to let her daughter take the shilling 'binding money'. There and then this transaction tied the child to working at the mill for the next ten or eleven years of her life.

Before long, however, the girl was in terror of the master's wife after being lashed soundly with a whip – which Mrs Newton always carried when checking the girls' bedroom – for appearing to laugh at her. The sufferings of the child's workmates meant that she was able to recall many of them by name for the rest of her life. For some, the published memoir is their only memorial.

There was Mary, savagely kicked by Newton himself for spilling some slops, after which 'a heavy sleepiness came over her, and she wore away and died'. A little London boy called Michael Wayland broke a horn and was thrust head-first into the earth closet. He was never the same after this and ran away, only to be found dead somewhere on the road to London.

Caroline Thompson was beaten until she lost her senses,

rescued too late by her mother who took her back to London where she spent the rest of her short life in a strait-jacket. Poor Betsy Witnough fell foul of Mrs Newton when she threw some bad bread away, being thrashed so hard by the master that she could not see through her swollen eyes, but was put back to work nevertheless. Her sufferings ended when she drowned in a pond after creeping outside for a drink of water, so parched that she actually risked leaving her machine.

Local tradition tells of so many deaths at Cressbrook and Litton mills in the early years that clandestine burials were shared between Taddington and Tideswell in unmarked graves. Official documentary evidence states that at least six Cressbrook apprentices died between 1803 and 1806. The death rate there from epidemics and accidents in later years was not considered unduly high – 1.3% between 1825 and 1835.

The memoirs confirm that decorum was fully observed between the apprentices, with the additional information that any girl caught talking to a boy had her head shorn, a punishment dreaded above all others. Not everyone, however, observed the supposed rules on modesty; older girls had a particular fear of being punished by Tom-the-Devil because he used to pull up their clothes and bend them over his knee to be spanked in full view of all the men and boys.

According to the woman's account, Newton encouraged such rough treatment. She too had endured beatings from Tom-the-Devil, so many on her head that her brother took his courage in his hands and complained to the master, who horse-whipped him for his insolence. She adds furthermore that she was also hit about the head by Newton himself, a beating which left her with sleeping problems for the rest of her life.

Both former apprentices asserted that they were always kept locked up when not working. City urchins who had been sent to Cressbrook with promises of sport among the hills and fishing in the streams found the disappointment all too much. Once in a while a few lads managed to get past the watchman and over the wall when work was done, but they were usually caught and paid with a lashing.

John tells how such escapades cost him several floggings at the hand of Newton, the most severe being about thirty heartfelt strokes across his bare buttocks as punishment for plucking a couple of roses from the master's garden one summer night. On the day that the lad dared to ask Newton whether he had finally served his time he was answered with a beating.

As for a good night's sleep in comfortable beds, those who had slept in them describe sharing with two others, or five others if the bed was a double. Although Mary Sterndale avoided the unladylike subject of lavatories, we learn from John that over two hundred boys shared only two or three 'necessaries'.

During his first year at Cressbrook, John started work at 6.00am on an empty stomach, breakfast being brought round to be eaten whilst working. To him the food compared favourably with what he had been given at Litton, but, perhaps because she was new to institution food, the girl found it revolting; the Derbyshire oatcake was coarse and sour and the meat in the pies was nothing more than thick chunks of boiled bacon fat. The children had to make time to clean and oil the machinery during their dinner hour.

That the Newtons had a reputation for exceeding the statutory 12 hour day is confirmed in the article on Cressbrook Mill by Miss M H Mackenzie. Her research also revealed that in 1816 William Newton's apprentices were almost certainly, and illegally, put to nightwork. Interestingly, the same author points out that Newton had probably been involved in introducing parish apprentices to Litton Mill during his partnership there. We further learn that prior to taking over at Cressbrook, Newton was working for a partner of Ellis Needham, the infamous owner of Litton Mill, whose cruelty towards his apprentices remains undisputed.

Since Miss Mackenzie revealed incriminating material in 'Cressbrook and Litton Mills 1779-1835', other writers have dispensed with their predecessors' cynicism towards the apprentices' memoirs. For, unfortunately, this type of publication has not always found a sympathetic ear. *A Memoir of Robert Blincoe*, for instance, was frequently dismissed as spiteful propaganda for the subsequent Factory Act of 1822, largely on grounds that the story of the illiterate Blincoe was 'ghost written' by a journalist.

Vignettes of Derbyshire is also now read with a more critical eye. Author Mrs Mary Sterndale was an educated lady who wrote in the style of her time; thus the Peak scenery became a 'fairyland', Hope Dale displayed 'all her sylvan graces', the Winnats Pass opened onto a vista of 'mountains standing like the flaming swords of the seraphims at the gates of Paradise' and Wardlow was an 'alpine village'. Indeed, fulsome praise was heaped on Derbyshire and everything in it.

On her travels Mary Sterndale condescended to talk to the obsequious 'peasantry' and approved the 'intellectual requirements of the Derbyshire rustics'. Compared with other contemporary observers, she was either unusually lucky in her choice of peasant story-tellers or she scanned them through rose-coloured spectacles.

Vignettes of Derbyshire is dedicated to, and contains effusive references to, the sculptor and artist Chantrey, he who drew the only known likeness of William Newton. He had become Sir Francis Chantrey by the time the book was published. The author drops other names which hint at a familiar artistic and literary circle. She mentions as a friend from her youth the Reverend Peter Cunningham, a writer and rector of Eyam who, incidentally, had introduced William Newton to Anna Seward. Flowery compliments are conferred on Miss Seward herself, to whom 'Genius opened wide her golden gates'. This somewhat vain lady poet basked in the soubriquet 'The Swan of Lichfield', although after her death her writings were to be described as 'absolutely execrable' by Sir Walter Scott, to whom she bequeathed her unpublished work.

It was Miss Seward who proclaimed her protege, William Newton, 'The Minstrel of the Peak'. In return for his humble and total adoration, the lady forgave what she saw as his inferior station in life, although she did once remark that 'till Mr Cunningham kindly distinguished him, he had associated only with the unlettered and the inelegant vulgar'. Deeply flattered by verse which Newton dedicated to her own literary brilliance (a gift obviously deserving wider recognition) she submitted the following lines to *The Gentleman's Magazine* on his behalf:

'I boast no aid from Phoebus or the Nine,
No sister Graces decorate my line,
The Spring Pierian never flowed for me,
Those dulcet waters were reserved for thee.'

As regards her own material published towards the end of her life, it has been shown that Anna Seward altered and embellished certain original letters, apparently to ensure a role for herself in literary history. The correspondence in question contained references to William Newton.

Those who wonder whether *Vignettes of Derbyshire* might have been a coterie production should also take a look at *Peak Scenery*, a major literary work published by Ebenezer Rhodes, also in 1824. The illustrations are by Chantrey, to whom part four was dedicated, Anna Seward is referred to as an 'eminent female' and Cunningham's poems are remembered 'with pleasure and affection'. Their mutual friend William Newton is 'an indulgent master', although Rhodes did deplore the 'moral-murdering system of congregating boys and girls together in the same factory . . . extensive in Derbyshire'.

It may be that two of these former inmates, deprived of their childhood and left in broken health, had seen the private face of their old master. Or they might in truth have been two embittered adults, encouraged by others to exaggerate their stories for political exploitation.

So which was the real William Newton, Minstrel of the Peak? Was he a rare enlightened exception in a disgraceful Dickensian system? For a century and a half his reputation remained unblemished and his kindness passed into legend. But this view was chiefly born from a lady's pen. If that pen had been dipped in honey to please mutual friends, did it perhaps refuse to record that William Newton was really just another cruel industrialist typical of his day?

Whichever he was, he had to answer to his own master in the end; as we are told in the Book of Proverbs. 'A good name is rather to be chosen than great riches . . .'.

BIBLIOGRAPHY

'Cressbrook and Litton Mills 1779-1835' by M H Mackenzie, in *Derbyshire Archaeological Journal*, 1968, **88**, pp.1-25.

'Cressbrook Mill 1810-1835' by M H Mackenzie, in *Derbyshire Archaeological Journal*, 1970, **90**, pp.60-70.

See also:

'Cressbrook and Litton Mills: an Alternative View' by S D Chapman, in *Derbyshire Archaeological Journal*, 1969, **89**, pp. 86-90.

'Cressbrook and Litton Mills: a Reply' by M H Mackenzie, in *Derbyshire Archaeological Journal*, 1970, **90**, pp.56-59.

CHAPTER 5

Little John's Grave? The Lawful Village Perch

by Brian Robinson

TRADITION WOULD HAVE US BELIEVE THAT LITTLE John was the lieutenant and faithful comrade of Robin Hood and was at length to bury the body of his deceased leader at Kirkless Park in Yorkshire. The legend continues that, whilst on his final journey, Little John saw the vale of Hathersage and exclaimed that this was the place where he should die and be buried. Descending into the vale, he reached the cottage which had once been his home, near the churchyard gate. Within this cottage, after a short while, he breathed his last and was buried in the nearby churchyard (see, however, note 1). Here, for several centuries, the local inhabitants have been all too ready to direct visitors to a plot of prodigious length which they claim is his grave. Indeed, Little John's grave in the churchyard at Hathersage was described as early as 1652, by Elias Ashmole, the celebrated Oxford antiquarian (Figure 1).

Such is the tale.

However, the *Dictionary of National Biography* tells us that neither Little John nor his leader Robin Hood ever walked the

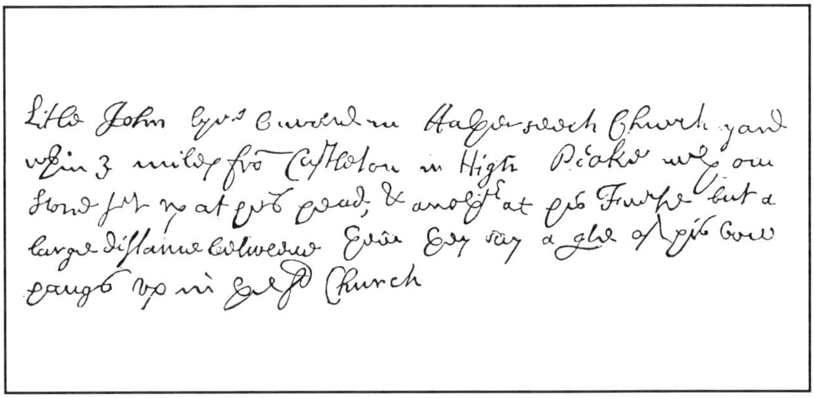
Litle John lyes buried in Hatherseech Church yard
within 3 miles fro Castleton in High Peake with one
Stone set up at his head, & another at his Feete but a
large distance betweene them They say a part of his bow
hangs up in the said Church

Figure 1. A facsimile of that part of the writings of Elias Ashmole, copied from his manuscripts at the University of Oxford, that relates to Little John's grave. It reads: 'Little John lyes buried in Hatherseech Church yard within 3 miles fro Castleton in High Peake with one Stone set up at his head, and another at his Feete but a large distance betweene them. They say a part of his bow hangs up in the said Church' (current source, Jewitt).

earth. Both are heroes of pagan mythology and creations of popular imagination, beautiful creations, no doubt, but not historical. Indeed, Robin Hood is distinguished by being accorded an article in the Dictionary devoted entirely to arguing that he never existed. Moreover, in 1989, J C Holt (page 7), in what may be regarded as a definitive study, writes: 'This book is about a legend [the proliferation of which is reflected in the widespread nature of Robin Hood place names] rather than a man. The legend began more than seven hundred years ago . . . He has survived as a hero in ballad, book, poem and play ever since'.

Amongst the plays in which, before the end of the fifteenth century, Robin and his men had become familiar dramatic characters, were those of the traditional May Day festivities. This could well explain, as suggested by Holt (page 58), and over a century ago by J Hunter, the hat (on a chain), the bow with some arrows, and, an unlikely accoutrement for a forester, a cuirass of chain armour, all of which have been claimed as having belonged to Little John and which hung in the church at Hathersage until all but the hat, which was apparently lost in the eighteenth century, were removed to Cannon Hall, near Barnsley (see note 2). Jenny Sherd, in her interview with Dr Spencer T Hall (see note 3), claimed that the cap, too, was taken to Cannon Hall, but Walter Spencer Stanhope, the owner of the Hall in 1877, is quoted by Dr J C Cox as stating, on 2 June 1876, that 'I never heard of any cap having been part of the relics of Little John which were brought to Cannon Hall, neither is there any such article now preserved here'.

Whatever may be the case regarding the cap's ultimate fate, it seems reasonable to assume that all the above-mentioned artifacts were simply the expensive ceremonial accoutrements of the Little John of the village's mediaeval May Day plays that, for safe-keeping, were kept in the church for the remainder of the year. Likewise, as suggested by Hunter, the cottage in Hathersage (note 3), which was believed by the villagers to have been that of Little John, may simply have been the abode of a man who had, on past occasions, impersonated the mythical hero in the plays, now discontinued and forgotten. With regard to the articles in the church, Miss Mary Andrews alternatively suggests that these, and in particular the bow, might have had some connection with a monument – near which the latter hung in the church – to the Eyres, a family renowned in the area and who held the official rank as Gentlemen Foresters whose members carried a longbow as their sign of office.

As long ago as 1822, E Rhodes poured ridicule upon the claim that the 'grave' is that of Little John, a sentiment also expressed by Holt (page 176), and suggested that it was merely the site of interment of the corpse of a tall man from the nearby settlement of Offerton.

Whether there were any human remains interred at all in the 'grave' is, in fact, open to speculation. According to James Pilkington, after several earlier excavations had failed to reveal any evidence for this, digging in 1784 to a greater depth uncovered an alleged human thigh bone some 29 inches long (the length of this bone has also been variously quoted as 28 inches (Charles Spencer Stanhope, in Cox), from 28 to 29 inches (the sexton's son, in Stirling) and 32 inches (Jenny Sherd, in Hall). Unfortunately, no trace of it now exists – a histopathological examination would have confirmed its anatomical authenticity, whatever that may have been, if nothing else. Amusingly, the bone would appear to have metamorphosed, for W B Gardner and A R H Moncrieff describe the remains which were disinterred from the 'grave' in the eighteenth century as 'a skeleton of uncommon size' – such is the stuff of legend! In fact, no reason has been offered as to why other skeletal remains were not discovered along with the alleged thigh bone, although an explanation for this may be sought in the report of an ostensible earlier opening of the 'grave' reported by Thomas Bateman, which reads: 'Dr. Moor, of Wakefield, who frequently came

Figure 2. A plan of Little John's grave, as drawn by W H Elgar in September 1919 (from Addy, page 209). By this time (cf Figure 3) the modern, equilaterally-arched headstone, clearly visible in Figure 4, had been erected.

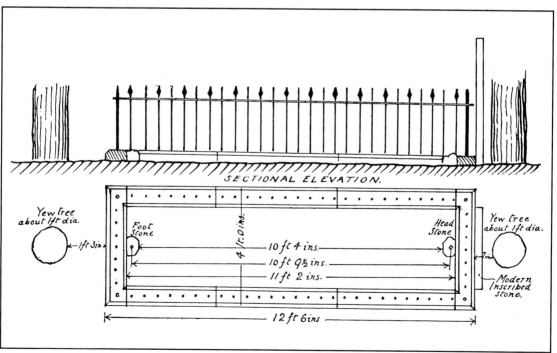

here [to Hathersage] to attend Mr Ashton, of Hathersedge Hall, in his last illness, about the year 1728 [Ashton actually died in 1725 – see note 2], caused it [the 'grave'] to be dug up. Nothing was found except bones of very great size, much larger than what is now found in graves, and having satisfied his curiosity, had it filled up again'.

If the 'grave' is not the final resting place of human remains, then what is it? Furthermore, even if it is, what might it have been beforehand?

The answer to these questions resides in an article by S O Addy that was published in 1925 (see note 4).

Addy affirms that the clue to the *raison d'être* of this site is the two ancient stones, noted since the writings of Ashmole (Figure 1), one at each end of its longitudinal extremities and each measuring some 5 x 7 inches in cross-section (Figure 2) and protruding a few inches above ground level. Of particular significance is the small depression present in a roughly central location on the upper surface of each of the two stones, as if to ensure a more accurate measurement by taking a line between their centres, a distance which, as will be seen, is extremely significant. In fact, in the illustration of the 'grave' by William Bray in 1793, these two stones were its only distinguishing features. This situation remained so at least until 1858, in which year Richard Keene noted 'Little John's grave was rather a disappointment in a photographic point of view, as it consisted only

Figure 3. Little John's grave, certainly later than 16 April 1905 – the date of the latest interment indicated on the grave stone at the far right – by which time the metal railings, but not the inscribed headstone, had been erected. The board on the post reads 'Little John's Grave Marked by Head Stone & Foot Stone Beneath the Yew Trees'.

68

Figure 4. Little John's grave circa 1935 showing, midway along its south side, the then recently erected stone that is inscribed 'The care of this grave was undertaken by the Ancient Order of Foresters Friendly Society June 24th 1929'. This is the last addition (see Figures 2 and 3) that, until now, has been made to the site.

of two very small stones at a very great distance apart, 'only this and nothing more". However, by circa 1905 the iron railings were in position (Figure 3), but the modern headstone (Figures 2 and 4) had still to be erected.

The distance between the two original stones is currently 10 feet 9½ inches (Figure 2), but it is clear that over the years these two stones have been moved closer together, a point previously noted by Cox and William Andrews. On 27 February 1685 (Old Style), Leonard Wheatcroft of Ashover noted that the grave was '14 foot in length'. John Wilson of Broomhead Hall, near Sheffield (1719-1783) stated 'Little John's Grave in Hathersage churchyard, at the back of the clerk's house, is distinguished by two small stones set up at each end, and is 4 yards 10 inches long betwixt stone and stone'. Bray stated that 'They [the stones] are 13 feet four inches distance'.

It seems reasonable to assume, on the basis of these three old measurements, that the distance between the mid-points of these two stones used to be about 13½ feet, the length of the perch by which the short acre of 3,240 square yards used to be measured. It thus seems very likely that what is now known as Little John's Grave was, in fact, originally established as the standard perch for Hathersage in mediaeval times.

The length of the perch varied between 9 and 26 feet (before it was eventually standardised at 16½ feet) and every village had its own lawful standard, since it was established by local arbitrary procedures. In one of these, which actually involved the church, sixteen men were taken as they happened to leave at the end of a Sunday service, and were stood in a row, foot to foot, behind each other (Figure 5), the length obtained being the local perch to be used for surveying purposes. This method would also explain the maintenance of the standard in the churchyard, also located conveniently near to the clerk's house, as noted by Wilson, in the situation at Hathersage.

By analogy with other parishes, Addy states (page 212) that 'If it could be shown that the arable lands in Hathersage were measured by a perch of 13½ feet... we should be sure that 'Little John's Grave' was the village perch'. Mediaeval land measurements in Hathersage do not seem yet to have been studied. However, Addy (page 219) also notes the probability 'that many of our old churches were laid out in accordance with local measures', states that he 'should like to see, for instance, an accurate measured plan of Hathersage church' and concludes that 'If by any chance it should be found that the nave of Hathersage church is 54 feet in length ... we may be sure that this measurement was composed of four perches of 13½ feet each'. The length of the nave of the Hathersage parish church is, indeed, approximately 54 feet, the equivalent of four perches each of 13½ feet or thereabouts, namely one Hathersage chain, set out about 1381.

From the Anglo-Saxon era through to the nineteenth century,

Figure 5. Establishing the village perch outside a church during the Middle Ages (from Addy, page 216).

mythical names, prevalently associated with giants, were given to objects whose significance had been lost. It would therefore be natural that, when their purpose as marking the standard for the village perch came to be forgotten, the two stones in Hathersage churchyard, as did a similar pair of stones at Penrith, began to be regarded as the headstone and footstone of a giant's grave. And what giant in Hathersage would then have been more deserving of such a final resting place than the legendary Little John, who, for so long, had been portrayed in a leading role in the May Day festivities of the village.

Little John's alleged grave in Hathersage is now confined to fiction, but, in return, the village has regained the reality of its mediaeval standard of surveying, its local perch. Surely a more than satisfactory exchange!

NOTES

1. An interesting variation concerning the death of Little John is presented by J A Walker, according to whom Little John's life was terminated on the gallows when he was executed, for a robbery, on Arbor Hill, Dublin. If this be so, it would appear to be very unlikely that his corpse was buried at Hathersage.

2. At the beginning of the eighteenth century, much of the land in Hathersage was owned by Benjamin Ashton. When he died, in 1725, his estate passed to his sister Christina, who, in 1715, had married William Spencer, of Cannon Hall, near Barnsley. It is recorded by A M W Stirling that it was William Spencer who caused the removal to Cannon Hall of the longbow, arrows and chain armour that hung in Hathersage parish church. On the other hand, Cox attributes the removal to William's son, John. Ann Spencer, John's younger sister, married Walter Stanhope and the Spencer-Stanhopes and their descendants retained possession of the bow. It eventually passed down to Elizabeth Frazer (nee Spencer-Stanhope), who had married George Frazer in 1920, and their son Simon had the bow at his home in Scotland in 1980. However, no trace of the arrows and chain armour remains, these artifacts being apparently lost during repairs to the Hall in 1870.

The above-mentioned John Spencer died unmarried in 1775 and thus the estates in Hathersage were inherited by his elder sister Christina who, in 1748, had married William Shuttleworth. It was their third son, James, who lived with his eldest brother, John, at Hathersage Hall, who had the alleged grave of Little John opened in 1784.

Stirling relates that although John Shuttleworth was angry at his younger brother having disturbed the grave, James Shuttleworth took the bone to show it to his cousin at Cannon Hall. Here, following a warning from an old huntsman that 'No good will come to either of ye so long as ye keep dead men's bones above ground', both young men suffered a series of serious accidents (the beginning of a legend within a legend?). Accidents, one of which was almost fatal, continued to beleaguer his cousin at Cannon Hall even after James returned to Hathersage with the bone, which he then kept hung above his bed at the Hall. James too, we are told, continued to be beset by accidents – two actually in the churchyard itself – and, whilst he was lying ill in bed, his nurse, seeing the hanging bone, echoed the old huntsman's warning. James, apparently unable to any longer withstand this pre-emptive Yorkshire-Derbyshire equivalent of the so-called 'Curse' of Tutankhamun, hurriedly ordered the village sexton to re-inter the bone. However, more than a year afterwards, during a visit made to Hathersage by his cousin in the company of one William Strickland, the latter, as a result of listening to the tale of the bone, sent for the sexton and offered him half-a-crown if he would disinter the ill-omened item and bring it to him. The bone, inside which was a particularly fine cobweb, was produced in a suspiciously short time, further enquiries establishing that the sexton had apparently ignored James Shuttleworth's earlier order, for he had for some time been secretly exhibiting the relic to curious strangers at sixpence per head. No doubt to the financial dismay of the sexton, Strickland retained his trophy, which he carried off into oblivion.

3. As a result of a visit that he made to the so-called Little John's cottage at Hathersage in 1841, Dr Spencer T Hall described it as 'a rustic and, doubtless, a very antiquated one, with exceedingly thick walls, built without lime' and stated that at the time of his visit 'it was half mantled with ivy and shaded by trees' and 'In it then lived Jenny Sherd'. Jenny told him that she was then seventy years old and had been born in the cottage, in which her father, William Bohem, who had died at the age of ninety-two twenty years earlier, had also lived from his youth. He, Jenny related, had received the assurance from his predecessors in the cottage at the time he began his tenancy that Little John had died there, and they, in turn, had received the same information sixty years before from those who had preceded them, and thus from mouth-to-mouth had the tradition descended from Little John's time. By 1858, Jenny was dead and by 1884 the cottage had been pulled down (Keene).

4. Regrettably, this well-researched article on 'this thing at Hathersage' has been ignored, either through ignorance or for convenience, by all but one of those who have subsequently written regarding the 'grave'. Most, including the latest, David Bell, in yet another compilation featuring the county's alleged apparitions, and John N Merrill (see note 5) simply sustain the legend. Unfortunately, too, the one reference to Addy's work, on page 50 of *Derbyshire Rambles*, an undated compilation of articles by W Jacques written for the *Derbyshire Times* during 1930, is devoid of any critical evaluation. It merely arbitrarily declares that the Ancient Order of Foresters, which had then recently acquired a vested interest in perpetuating the legend by taking over the grave's care (Figure 4) (a nice gesture but hardly proof positive, as regarded by some, that little John really existed), visit it 'annually with bands and regalia' and 'pooh-pooh the 'perch' [Addy's] theory and stick to Little John' – hardly an erudite conclusion.

5. The latest gilding on the Little John tale was added in 1993 when John N Merrill, referring to Hathersage and the so-called Robin Hood's Stoop, states, without comment or criticism, that 'The latter is said [by whom?] to be the place where Little John fired an arrow which landed one and a half miles away in the churchyard'. Some weapon!! But such is the might of myth.

BIBLIOGRAPHY

Addy, S O, 'Little John's Grave', and the Lawful Village Perch', in *Journal of the Derbyshire Archaeological and Natural History Society*, 1925, **47**, pp.206-221.

Andrews, Mary, *Long Ago in Peakland* (R Milward & Sons Ltd, Nottingham; 1948), pp.57, 58.

Andrews, William, *Bygone Derbyshire* (Frank Murray, Hull; William Andrews & Co, Hull; Simpkin, Marshall, Hamilton, Kent & Co, London; 1892), p.248.

Bateman, Thomas, *Ten Years Digging* (quoted by Addy, p.207).

Bell, David, *Derbyshire Ghosts and Legends* (1993), pp.61, 62.

Bray, William, *Sketch of a Tour into Derbyshire and Yorkshire* (White, London; 1783), p.245 and plate V (opposite p.208).

Cox, J Charles, *Notes on the Churches of Derbyshire* (Palmer and Edmunds, Chesterfield; Bemrose and Sons, London and Derby; 1877), vol.2, pp.236-239.

Gardner, W B and Moncrieff, A R H, *The Peak Country* (Adam and Charles Black, London; 1908), p.107.

Hall, Spencer T, *The Peak and the Plain* (Houlston and Stoneman, London; 1853), pp.32-36.

Holt, J C, *Robin Hood* (Thames and Hudson Ltd, London; 1989).

Hunter, J, *The Great Hero of the Ancient English Minstrelsy of England: Robin Hood* (London, 1852; Worksop, 1883), p.69.

Jewitt, Llewellynn, *The Ballads & Songs of Derbyshire* (Bemrose and Lothian, London; Bemrose and Sons, Derby; 1867), p.92.

Keene, Richard, 'A Six Days' Ramble over Derbyshire Hills and Dales, in the Year 1858', in *Journal of the Derbyshire Archaeological and Natural History Society*, 1884, **6**, pp.109-156 (see p.139).

Merrill, John N, *Derbyshire Folklore* (Trail Crest Publications Ltd, Winster; 1993), pp.35, 36.

Pilkington, James, *A View of the Present State of Derbyshire* (J Drewry, Derby; 1789), vol.II, p.386.

Rhodes, E, *Peak Scenery, or Excursions in Derbyshire* (Longman, Hurst, Rees, Orme, Brown, John Murray, and Messrs Rodwell and Martin, London; Mr E Rhodes, Sheffield; 1822), part III, p.8.

Stirling, A M W, *Annals of a Yorkshire House* (John Lane, London and New York; 1911), vol.2, pp.62-70.

Walker, J A, 'Memoir on the Armour and Weapons of the Irish', annexed to *Historical Essay on the Dress of the Ancient and Modern Irish* (quoted by Rhodes, E, *Peak Scenery; or, the Derbyshire Tourist* (Longman, Hurst, Rees, Orme, Brown, and Green, London; the author, Sheffield; 1824), p.180).

Wheatcroft, Leonard; the Autobiography of, in *Journal of the Derbyshire Archaeological and Natural History Society*, 1899, **21**, p.46.

Wilson, John, in Bateman, Thomas, *Ten Years Digging* (quoted by Addy, p.210).

CHAPTER 6

Forgive Us Our Trespassers

by Roland Smith

IN RAMBLERS' MYTHOLOGY, THE 1932 MASS TRESPASS on Kinder Scout – sometimes known as the Battle of Kinder Scout – has the equivalent status of a Waterloo.

Variously described as an important catalyst for the National Parks and access to the countryside movement, or a brief scrap between ramblers and gamekeepers which actually put back the cause of access by 20 years, the events of that fine Spring afternoon over 60 years ago simply refuse to be forgotten.

Every significant anniversary of the event since the 50th in 1982 has been celebrated by marches, re-enactments and speeches by access activists. The original trespassers, five of whom served terms of imprisonment for their part in the incident, are ironically now lauded as martyrs to the access cause – having been firmly ostracised by the official rambling movement at the time.

What then is the truth behind the apparent contradictions of this most famous, or infamous, of the many trespasses which took place on Peak District moorland and every moorland during the rambling boom of the 1930s?

The Myth
PEAK TRESPASS PROTEST – MOB LAW ON THE MOORS – *Manchester Evening Chronicle*

SUNDAY'S ATTACK ON KINDER – *Manchester Evening News*

MASS TRESPASS ARRESTS ON KINDER SCOUT – FREE FIGHT WITH GAMEKEEPERS ON MOUNTAIN – AMAZING SCENES IN MOORLAND VILLAGE – *Daily Despatch, Manchester*.

The florid newspaper headlines of the time graphically tell the story. The accompanying reports were full of descriptions of a 'free fight' and 'melee' between stick-wielding gamekeepers and a large body of unarmed ramblers on the western slopes of the Peak's reigning summit, Kinder Scout. It was all good, open-air, escapist copy in those dark days of the Thirties Depression, when, as now, a walk on the moors was the only salvation for thousands of unemployed people trapped in the surrounding dingy industrial cities all week.

'The Battle of Kinder Scout', as the event was first described in a BBC2 documentary film in 1970, was the successful culmination of a century-long campaign to free the Peak District moors from the yoke of land-grabbing owners, enabling the rambling public to wander freely across their peaty summits. That long-standing right had been stolen from them by grasping landlords who, about a hundred years before, had enclosed the once freely-accessible 'King's Land' for their grouse rearing and sheep grazing.

Frustrated by the official rambling federations' lack of success in restoring the public's 'right to roam' through negotiation, walkers from the surrounding cities made the spontaneous response of the mass trespass to the 'Forbidden Mountain' of Kinder Scout, in order to win back what they believed was theirs by right.

Figure 1. The trespassers set out from Hayfield in the early afternoon of Sunday, 24 April 1932 (Reproduced by courtesy of the Peak National Park).

So it was that on Sunday, 24 April 1932 a large crowd of ramblers gathered on the Recreation Ground in the little gritstone village of Hayfield at the foot of the Kinder Road which led to their 'Holy Grail' – the 2,088ft (636m) summit of Kinder Scout. Large numbers of police mingled with them, intent on preserving public order. The crowd, estimated at up to 1,000 people, moved off up Kinder Road to the disused quarry at Bowden Bridge for a rally.

Here the ringleader, a 20-year-old unemployed motor mechanic named Bernard Rothman, addressed the assembled throng. From his rocky pulpit, he told them that despite the stories in the media, they were not hooligans intent on trouble, but peaceful demonstrators who would not be stopped from exercising their right to roam.

The laughing, singing group then moved off up the Kinder Road and onto the path up White Brow, round Nab Brow above the glittering waters of the Kinder Reservoir and into William Clough. Part way up the clough, at a given signal, the crowd of ramblers suddenly turned off the path and started to scramble up the forbidden slopes of Sandy Heys in open formation.

About halfway up the steep, tussocky slope, groups of gamekeepers numbering about 20-30 in all, emerged waving sticks and shouting to the ramblers to stop and turn back. The ramblers took no notice, and scuffles occurred between the two groups, resulting in a temporary keeper, Edward Beevers, being knocked to the ground and injuring an ankle. Other keepers had their sticks forcibly taken from them.

The ramblers marched on to the top of the slope and onto the summit of Kinder Scout, where a victory meeting was held after they met up with another group of Sheffield ramblers who had made their trespass unopposed from the Edale side.

Heads held high, the trespassers marched back down into Hayfield, where six of the leaders were arrested and thrown into Hayfield Lock-up before being incarcerated at New Mills Police Station overnight.

At the subsequent trial of the defendants at Derby Assizes, much was made of the fact that they had 'foreign-sounding' names – a reference which was interpreted as evidence of the anti-semitism which was rife at the time. One of the defendants was also found to have a copy of a book by Lenin in his possession. To the general amusement of the court, Judge Sir Edward Acton innocently remarked: 'Isn't that the Russian gentleman?'.

Five of the defendants were imprisoned for terms of up to six months on charges ranging from occasioning grievous bodily harm to riotous assembly – and the myth of the Mass Trespass was born.

The Truth

In his published account of the 1932 Kinder Trespass, one of the leaders, Benny Rothman, admitted that 'a whole mythology has grown around the Trespass'. As the years go by and memories become more and more indistinct, some of the facts were bound to become distorted, yet at every anniversary, more 'survivors' seem to appear, and the myth continues to grow.

Far from being a spontaneous manifestation of ramblers' frustration at the lack of progress on access negotiations, the 1932 Mass Trespass was a carefully orchestrated political protest. It was organised by the Lancashire branch of the British Workers' Sports Federation, a working-class movement affiliated to the Communist Party.

It arose after some members of the Federation with their guests from London had been turned back from a walk on Bleaklow during Easter 1932 by a group of irate gamekeepers. The BWSF, of which Benny Rothman was the Lancashire district secretary, resolved to force the issue by calling out as many ramblers as they could for a showdown with the keepers.

According to the late Tom Stephenson, secretary of the Ramblers' Association for 20 years and a life-long campaigner for access, the BWSF was an 'ephemeral' body, made up of men not known to have shown any previous interest in the access problem and who did not play any further part in the subsequent campaign.

The event was well-publicised by the BWSF in advance by interviews in Manchester newspapers, leaflets and even chalked notices on pavements which advertised the event.

But it was immediately denounced by the rambling establishment of the day. Both the Manchester and Sheffield Ramblers' Federations condemned the proposed action, claiming that it would prejudice their constitutional efforts for access by negotiation with the owners. They urged their members to have nothing to do with it, although many did, in fact, take part.

The number of ramblers who took part was also grossly exaggerated, a not uncommon occurrence at open-air gatherings. According to *The Manchester Guardian*, which sent a reporter to the event, the figure was between 400 and 500, while the prosecution at the trial estimated it at between 150 and 200.

Although he helped organise the publicity for the trespass, Benny Rothman was only one of the leaders, and his inspirational speech at Bowden Bridge Quarry was only made on the spur of the moment after a more senior speaker had failed to show up.

But the greatest myth of all associated with the 1932 Mass

Figure 2. William Clough, scene of the "trespass" (Reproduced by courtesy of the Peak National Park).

Trespass, according to Tom Stephenson, was the fact that the trespassers hardly trespassed at all. They certainly did not get within two miles of the 'forbidden summit' of Kinder Scout, and their victory meeting was held on a public path at Ashop Head, where Stephenson's great monument of the Pennine Way crosses between Kinder and Mill Hill.

The path which the trespassers took up William Clough was the right of way between Hayfield and the Snake Inn which had been successfully negotiated by the Hayfield and Kinder Scout Ancient Footpaths Society as long ago as 1897. It had been open for unobstructed public use since then.

According to the *Guardian* correspondent, the advance guard of the trespassers first saw the keepers – about eight of them – as they ascended William Clough. At the pre-arranged signal, about 40 ramblers dropped down to the stream and started to climb up the slopes of Sandy Heys. There was a brief parley with the keepers, after which the scuffle started – 'it was not even a struggle', according to the journalist.

The outnumbered keepers were quickly disarmed, and some of the ramblers stayed to give assistance to the injured keeper Beevers. The rest, according to the *Guardian* reporter who was with them, turned left and rejoined the Hayfield-Snake Inn footpath for the victory meeting which was held at Ashop Head. This was confirmed by John Watson, one of the total of 17 keepers on the hill that day, who wrote later: 'We could hear them cheering and yelling as if they had achieved something, when they had achieved nothing at all. They only trespassed about 100 yards – never got more than half way up the clough'.

Rothman later agreed with Stephenson on the occasion of the making of the BBC2 film that the victory meeting with the Sheffield contingent was held at Ashop Head, 400 feet below and two miles north-west of Kinder's summit.

The Effect

After the Mass Trespass of 1932, leading ramblers and access campaigners like Harold Wild of Manchester, Stephen Morton of Sheffield and Fred Heardman of Edale were to claim that it had put back any hopes of access by 20 years.

Edward Royce, access secretary of the Manchester Federation, damned with faint praise. 'The year 1932 will not be remembered as a red letter year for the rambler', he wrote soon afterwards. 'It has been a period of more than the usual froth and bubble'. The Sheffield Clarion Ramblers, who were walking between Grindleford and Bamford on the day of the trespass, were equally dismissive in their 1933-34 Handbook. 'The Mass

Trespass on Kinder, if it did nothing else, threw a little more illumination on the subject (of access to mountains)'. But later in the same edition, editor G H B Ward was to claim that the 'savage' sentences imposed on the five defendants 'did not bring laurels to the other side', and reported that they had aroused rambling federations throughout the country to support the current Access to Mountains Bill.

Philip Daley of the Manchester Federation, a former chairman of the Ramblers' Association and chairman of the Access and Footpaths Committee of the Peak National Park authority for 19 years, was to be closely involved with the negotiations for access agreements with landowners in the Peak when the National Park was set up in 1951. Such agreements now cover over 80 square miles of the National Park, including Kinder Scout.

He wrote on the occasion of the 50th anniversary of the trespass that it had always been used as an argument against public access. 'Such public access as we have gained owes nothing whatever to the mass trespass organised by the British Workers' Federation, and I can say quite categorically and without fear of contradiction that the 'mass trespass' was a positive hindrance and deterrent to the discussion and negotiations to secure the freedom of the hills'.

Was the 1932 Mass Trespass really the greatest single event in the history of the campaign for access to mountain and moorland, or was it merely a well-publicised diversionary skirmish in a long-running war?

With the benefit of hindsight it seems that it was not the action of the trespassers which effectively united the campaign for access, but the severity of the sentences handed out to them. Perhaps due credit has never been given to the judge, Sir Edward Acton, whose Draconian verdicts unwittingly galvanised the access cause and created the first trespass martyrs.

BIBLIOGRAPHY

Daley, Philip, 'The Kinder Scout Mass Trespass', in *Rucksack Magazine*, June 1982.

Hill, Howard, *Freedom to Roam. The Struggle for Access to Britain's Moors and Mountains* (Moorland, Ashbourne; 1980).

Joad, C E M, *The Untutored Townsman's Invasion of the Country* (Faber & Faber, London; 1946).

Rothman, Benny, *The 1932 Kinder Trespass* (Willow Publishing, Altrincham; 1982).

Royce, Edward, 'Federation Notes', in *Manchester and District Ramblers' Federation Handbook*, 1933, pp.85, 87 and 133.

Sculthorpe, Harold, *Freedom to Roam* (Freedom Press, London; 1993).

Smith, Roland, 'Mass Trespass', in *The Great Outdoors Magazine*, April 1992, pp.59-63.

Stephenson, Tom, 'Kinder Scout Mass Trespass', in *Rucksack Magazine*, Autumn 1979, pp.8-9.

Stephenson, Tom, *Forbidden Land, The Struggle for Access to Mountain and Moorland* (Manchester University Press; 1989).

Ward, G H B, *Sheffield Clarion Ramblers' Handbook*, 1933-34, pp.134 and 185.

CHAPTER 7

Drowning Some Legends
of The Upper Derwent Valley

by Brian Robinson

Birchinlee, where are you now?

THE DERWENT VALLEY WATER ACT 1899, WHICH received the Royal Assent on 9 August in that year, incorporated the Derwent Valley Water Board (DVWB) – comprising representatives from the Corporations of Derby, Leicester, Nottingham and Sheffield and the County Council of Derbyshire – with powers to construct specified dams in the Ashop and Derwent Valleys, together with the associated delivery aqueducts. As modified by the Derwent Valley Water Act 1901, the first of the three proposed instalments of this work was to involve the construction of the Howden and Derwent Dams, and the delivery systems from their impounded reservoirs. Excavations began for the Howden Dam's foundations on 16 July 1901 and the dam was formally opened, amidst much grandeur, on 5 September 1912. In contrast, the Derwent Dam, for which the foundation excavations had begun on 18 July 1902, was commissioned some four years later than that at Howden with no formality whatsoever, a reflection of Britain's preoccupation at that time with the First World War.

The majority of the DVWB's manual labour force, in common with other such groups employed upon the construction of public works around the turn of the nineteenth century, were drawn from a group of men known as navvies. Their name evolved from the navigators, the workmen who had been responsible for the digging and construction of the navigations (canals) in earlier times. These men, from whose sweat and toil the engineers took the glory and the entrepreneurs took the profit, were a nomadic group who, along with their families, were estimated in 1908 to number about one hundred thousand persons. They moved about from one public work to another, an itinerant labour force whose gross abuse by employers was widespread.

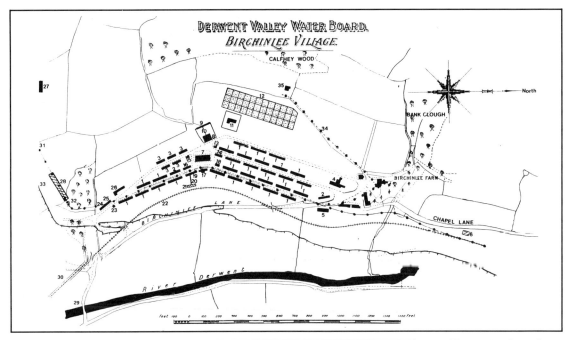

Figure 1. Plan of
Birchinlee, the
workmen's village
of the DVWB.

1 Workmen's huts for ten men, a hut keeper, his wife and his family.	18 Public bath-house.
2 Foremen's huts.	19 Derwent Canteen.
3 Huts for married workmen.	20 Pathway from the station platform to the cellar of the Derwent canteen.
4 General accident hospital.	21 Station platform.
5 Village coal store.	22 Bamford and Howden Railway.
6 Rubbish dump and incinerator.	23 Sweet and Tobacco shop (No 37A).
7 Recreation hall.	24 Missioner's house.
8 School (and mission) room.	25 Village inspector's house (No 40).
9 School playsheds.	26 Police station.
10 School playground, the left side being for the boys and the right side being for the girls.	27 Isolation hospital.
	28 Sewage Treatment plant.
	29 Ouzelden Bridge.
11 Schoolmaster's house.	30 Ouzelden Viaduct (the 'gantry').
12 Allotment gardens.	31 Course of the present road.
13 Greengrocers shop (No 66).	32 Sutton's Corner on the present road.
14 Clothier and draper (No 57).	33 Level of the Derwent Reservoir when it is full.
15 Cobbler and hairdresser (No 55).	34 Present private road to 35.
16 Post Office (No 26).	35 Gamekeeper's house (erected in 1909-10 and still in use).
17 Grocer's shop (No 21).	

Legislative action concerning the plight and exploitation of this workforce was long overdue when the situation was eventually brought to the attention of a select committee of the House of Commons which published its report in July 1846. This report had little, or no, immediate effect, but the working and living conditions of the navvies did gradually improve, changes which can be attributed to several factors, including the improvement in the general standard of living, the pressure of public opinion and the influence exerted by such organisations as the Navvy Mission Society. Nevertheless, even as late as 1908 it was estimated that some hundreds of navvies were still sleeping in haystacks, straw-yards, cowsheds, hen-houses and pigsties, or even completely out in the open, leading to their moral and physical deterioration.

Public building works usually necessitated the temporary immigration into the area of a body of men, some with wives and children. Dam construction sites particularly were situated in remote and mountainous localities, far from towns and villages where accommodation might be available or where new housing might be built by the contractors for lease to their employees.

This was the situation facing the DVWB with regard to the housing of the navvies who were to be employed in the construction of the Howden and Derwent Dams. Indeed, under Section 64 of the Derwent Valley Water Act 1899 it had a statutory obligation to provide a satisfactory environment for the care and accommodation of its employees. In conformity with this, the Board decided to erect a temporary village between the two construction sites. This village, situated about half a mile to the south of the Howden site, was named Birchinlee since it was built on land forming part of a farm by that name. The village was laid out around two main through-streets and a minor street, a cul-de-sac. The roads were well laid, kerbed, with footpaths, and illuminated at night by means of paraffin lamps. The domestic accommodation, in common with other buildings in the village, had corrugated iron outside walls and roofs, a feature that earned Birchinlee the widely-used nickname of 'Tin Town' or 'Tin City'. The buildings were all single storey, located on terraces on each side of the long straight sections of the two through-streets and on the bottom side of the minor street. The village (Figures 1, 2 and 3) also had shops, a school, two hospitals and a large and well-stocked recreation hall, and was supplied with a good water supply (from a nearby specially-created small reservoir) and modern sanitation. It was also served by a station – on the Bamford to Howden Railway, a standard gauge line of some seven-and-a-half miles that was constructed by the DVWB primarily for the transportation of building and other requisite materials to the two dam construction sites.

The DVWB admirably fulfilled its responsibility in the building and maintenance of Birchinlee village. It was a thriving and self-contained community: by early 1903 its population had reached 600, from late 1905 until mid-1912 it stood between 800 and 950 – reaching a maximum of 967 in August 1909, but then gradually began to fall as the construction works at the

Howden and then the Derwent sites neared completion. The dismantling and sale of the buildings and other village artifacts began during late 1912 and was almost completed by early 1915, at which time the remaining village residents, the village missioner and his five children, left. Nevertheless, and irrespective of the level of the adjacent Derwent Reservoir, the foundations of many of its public buildings, the sites of its terraces and railway station, the course of the railway in the vicinity (including the stone foundation of the nearby Ouzelden Viaduct, when the level of the Derwent Reservoir permits), and the remains of the village incinerator can still be readily located and distinguished with the help of a plan (see Figure 1), although it should be borne in mind that some of these sites now lie on private land belonging to Severn-Trent Water Ltd.

During 1928, Britain was subjected to a severe drought; a manifestation of this in the upper reaches of the Derwent Valley was reported on 18 October in the *Sheffield Daily Telegraph* as follows:

'Several thousand million gallons of water have disappeared during the last few months from the Derwent reservoir, which, when opened just before the war [the reservoir was, in fact, brought into use in 1916, namely *during* the First World War (*vide supra*)], inundated the village of Birchin Lee, and until yesterday, when the rains of the past few days began to have the effect of slowly refilling the huge lake, there was every prospect

Figure 2. Looking northward along the top through-road at Birchinlee on 2 September 1909. At the far left foreground is the school building, in the mid-foreground can be seen the roof, surmounted by a dome-like structure, of the recreation hall and, at the immediate left at the far end of the road, the general (accident) hospital is clearly discernable. In the background is the partially-built Howden Dam.

Figure 3. Looking southward down the Derwent Valley and across the village of Birchinlee circa 1910. The course of the Bamford and Howden Railway can be clearly discerned as it passes to the immediate eastern side of the village, crosses the Ouzelden Viaduct and continues onward toward its terminus at Thornhill.

of a shortage of water in Sheffield, Nottingham, Leicester and Derby.

Birchin Lee has come back to life in the last few weeks, cottage walls re-appearing like skeletons of a forgotten past. The roofs have been swept away by the thousands of tons of water which have kept them covered for more than a decade at a depth never less than 10ft, and more generally 30ft.... One of the water bailiffs told me, 'I have seen the water very low before, but never have the old cottages and the stone bridge shown'.'

The article was accompanied by a photograph of the village captioned 'The tiny village of 'Tin Town' [*vide supra*] before it was submerged under Derwent reservoir. Consequent upon the depletion of water in the reservoir recently, a glimpse of the submerged village has been obtained', and of the bridge in question, the Ouzelden Bridge, captioned 'THE BRIDGE which formerly carried the road from Derwent to the Ashop Valley [this is also utter nonsense], and which was submerged when the reservoir at Derwent, near Bamford, was filled, has once more become visible owing to the low level of water in the reservoir'.

Some forty-seven years later similar views were again expressed in the local press, this time the *South Yorkshire Times*, which on Saturday, 29 November 1975 carried a feature story

Figure 4. Three girls from the nearby village of Birchinlee standing by the Ouzelden Bridge circa 1910. The photograph was taken looking westward, and part of the village can just be discerned in the right background.

Figure 5. Some of the children from the nearby village of Birchinlee posing for their photograph, taken looking eastward, on the Ouzelden Bridge circa 1910. The buildings of Shire Owlers can just be discerned in the background in the gap between the trees.

on its page 55 by Audrey K Waterworth entitled 'A lost village is recalled' and beginning:

'The prolonged drought following the long, hot summer which has drained the reservoirs [Howden, Derwent and Ladybower] and brought tourists flocking to see the remains of the drowned villages of Derwent and Ashopton, has also revived memories of another village which lies beneath the waters of Derwent Dam.

This is Birchinlee, . . .'

The article was repeated, in view of widespread public interest, in the *South Yorkshire Times* of 4 September 1976 and, with regard to a related 'mini-exhibition' that was to be held at the Sheffield City Library during the summer of 1977, was

Figure 6. Looking eastward at the Ouzelden Bridge as exposed consequent upon the drop in the level of the Derwent Reservoir during the severe drought on the summer of 1947 (reproduced by courtesy of Mr J A Bullivant).

Figure 7. Looking eastward across the Derwent Valley at the village of Derwent circa 1910. In the foreground – in front of the church – is the school, and the large building standing high and to the left of the church is the vicarage. Derwent Hall (Figure 8) was some 200 yards from the church and to the village's immediate north.

referred to in the edition of 5 February 1977 (page 2) that reads '. . . Birchinlee, the lost village which now lies under the waters of Derwent Dam'.

Such is the stuff of legend, but what drivel! For although the Ouzelden Bridge (Figures 1, 4 and 5) was, indeed, exposed during the droughts of 1928 and 1947 (Figure 6), the village of

Figure 8. Looking eastward at the front elevation of Derwent Hall circa 1920.

Figure 9. Looking north-eastward across the Derwent Valley at the village of Ashopton circa 1920. The Ashopton Inn (Figure 10) is at the far left. The village site now lies deep below the Ladybower Reservoir to the immediate south-east of the present Ashopton Viaduct.

Birchinlee is no Peak District Brigadoon with sporadic re-appearances dependent upon the level of the water in the Derwent Reservoir, for the site and remaining foundations of the village lie well above the top water level of the reservoir. The reporters were obviously unfamiliar with the area (see Note 1) and it would appear that they had committed the cardinal error of permitting their pens to be directed by unsubstantiated local hearsay, such as the reminiscences of the water bailiff. However, they are not alone in their blunder, for many before and since have likewise based their writings upon uncorroborated local rumour and hype, even when authentication to the contrary was available. Such is also the situation regarding the association between the Howden and Derwent Dams, and their impounded reservoirs, and the 617 Squadron of the RAF (the Dambusters).

Figure 10. The Ashopton Inn circa 1907.

The Dambuster connection

From early in the Second World War, consideration had been given to various methods by which, through aerial attack, dams in Germany's industrial heartland might be breached. Leading the work was Barnes Wallis. Conventional bombing was ruled out, as was the use of torpedoes, since the target dams were protected by anti-torpedo nets. However, laboratory testing established the feasibility of the concept of a bouncing bomb, or, more accurately, a bouncing depth-charge. This, when released from an aircraft maintained under carefully controlled conditions, namely speed, height above water level and distance from the dam, would skip across the surface of a reservoir and come to rest against the immediate upstream side of the dam, which it would then rupture by sinking to a predetermined depth before exploding. The go-ahead for the full scale testing of such a weapon was given to Wallis on 4 December 1942 and, on 18 March 1943, 'X' Squadron RAF Bomber Command, six days later redesignated 617 Squadron, was formed. It consisted of 21 aircraft and 147 aircrew that were posted from main force squadrons throughout Lincolnshire, and from No 5 Group Bomber Command. Of the six dams that were earmarked for attack, the two main targets were the Moehne and Sorpe Dams, both of which had to be breached in order to maximise

industrial damage.

The weapons for this mission, the bouncing depth-charges, were cylindrical in shape. Each had a diameter of 50 inches, a length of 59⅞ inches, a total weight of 9,250 pounds, which included 6,600 pounds of Torpex underwater explosive, and contained three hydrostatic detonators set to activate at a depth of 30 feet and one self-destructive detonator set to act 90 seconds after release from the aircraft. They were to be carried by Lancaster bombers, one per aircraft, the under-fuselage of which had been modified by the fitting of a harness and a mechanism by which the bombs could be made to rotate along their axis. They were to be released back-spinning at 500 revolutions per minute from an aircraft flying at night directly toward the target dam at 232 miles per hour at a distance of 400 yards from it and precisely 60 feet above the surface of the reservoir.

Ingeniously simple methods were developed for maintaining the necessary exact altitude over the reservoir at night and for range-finding. The aircrews learned the use of these in seven weeks of intensive training during which they mastered the difficult art of precision navigation while flying at very low altitude at night, an essential prerequisite for the raid that was to take place during the night of 16-17 May 1943.

Figure 11. The last remaining operational Lancaster bomber flies over the Derwent Dam on 16 May 1988, at the unveiling of a plaque (Figure 12) inside the dam's west gateway, commemorating the overnight attack of 16-17 May 1943 by 19 Lancasters of 617 Squadron RAF on dams in western Germany.

Figure 12. The plaque, situated inside the west gateway of the Derwent Dam, that was unveiled on 16 May 1988.

Figure 13. The memorial, situated inside the west gateway of the Derwent Dam, that was unveiled on 2 October 1986.

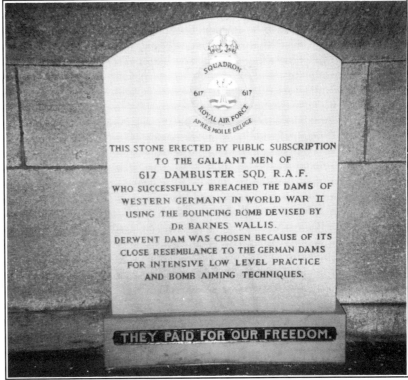

On 16 May 1988, the only remaining operational Lancaster bomber flew over the Derwent Dam (Figure 11) at the unveiling of a plaque (Figure 12) inside the dam's west gateway to commemorate the raid which, in the event, was to involve only 19

of the original 21 Lancaster bombers. The concluding words on a nearby memorial (Figure 13), that had been unveiled during a similar fly-past on 2 October 1986, read 'Derwent Dam was chosen because of its close resemblance to the German dams for intensive low level practice and bomb-aiming techniques' – but how many of the squadron's crews actually used the dam for practice and what was the nature of this practice?

The definitive book on the raid, which covers the story of the mission from its conception to the raid itself and the aftermath, was written by Dr John Sweetman, Head of the Department of Political and Social Studies at the Royal Military Academy, Sandhurst, and an historian formally educated at the Universities of Oxford and London. Despite the fact that this work, *The Dams Raid: Epic or Myth. Operation Chastise*, first appeared as long ago as 1980, the story of the raid, including the Derwent Dam's role in it, remains surrounded by legend and embroidered with many inaccuracies. One of the latter, aided and abetted by an ill-informed mass media and local hype, has been the widespread portrayal and acceptance by the public of the Derwent Reservoir as the major, or even the sole, training area for 617 Squadron, in point of fact far from the truth. The story is sometimes even compounded by further nonsense to the effect that bombs (presumably dummies, although even these would have damaged the dam had they impacted with it) were actually bounced across the reservoir during practice flights. For example, the reverse of a currently available postcard produced by 'Pedley' from a photograph by D Broadbent of the 16 May 1988 fly-past reads 'It was here that the Barnes Wallis 'Bouncing Bomb' was secretly tested prior to the Ruhr Valley raids on the Moehne and Eder Dams'. An earlier postcard, by 'Dennis', from the camera of the same photographer of the 2 October 1986 fly-past, reads 'It was here that secret practice in dropping the Barnes Wallis' [sic] bouncing bomb was carried out prior to the raid on the Moehne and Eder dams in the Ruhr Valley'.

In fact, the official papers on the raid, as used by Dr Sweetman, make very little reference to the area. The odd voice has been raised locally, apparently for the convenience of allusion and delusion, claiming that much of the information about the raid was not logged and that some papers relating to it were destroyed in a flood at 617 Squadron's headquarters. However, be this as it may, it is far from obvious how such 'negatives' might substantiate the local rumour, hearsay and hype, all of which are almost totally discredited by the official extant records.

Dropping trials and practice with the bouncing depth-charges had no connection whatsoever with the Derwent Valley. Initially, these were carried out off the Dorset coast. Then they were transferred to a bombing range in the Thames estuary, off the north Kent coast at Reculver, and finally, for security reasons, to a range some five miles off Broadstairs.

Regarding the training of the aircrews in the necessary low altitude night flying, nine stretches of water, of which the Derwent Reservoir was but one, were noted as being suitable. To begin with, all twenty crews then in the squadron used normal ground targets at the Wainfleet bombing range in the Wash. Then, on 6 May 1943 – ten days before the raid – specific practice areas were allocated. The Abberton Reservoir, three miles south of Colchester, and the Eyebrook Reservoir, two miles south of Uppingham, were used by nine crews in training for the attacks on the Eder and Moehne Dams respectively, the only dams that were, as a matter of fact, to be breached in the raid. Of the remaining crews, five were to form a mobile reserve, to provide back-up or to attack secondary targets; they practised over the Wash. It was only the remaining six crews who rehearsed in the Derwent Valley. In the event, on the night of the raid there were only five aircraft available for this group allocated to attack the Sorpe Dam. This dam differed from the Eder and Moehne Dams – which were masonry structures each with a pair of towers similar to the Howden and Derwent Dams – in that it consisted of a watertight core of concrete ten metres thick buttressed by high stabilising banks of earth covered with stone slabs that sloped away at an angle on both the upstream and downstream faces. It also lacked the towers which on the two other dams had been essential in the range-finding necessary for the modus operandi by which they had been attacked. The Sorpe Dam was therefore attacked not at a right angle to but *along* its length and by dropping the depth-charges in the more conventional manner, namely without back-spin or intentional bouncing, near to its upstream face. In the event, only two bombers reached this target and, although it was hit, the Sorpe Dam, most likely because of its concrete core, was not breached, a major setback to the overall effect of the raid.

On only two other occasions would it appear that practice flights were made in the Derwent Valley. The first of these was on 28 March 1943 when the Squadron Leader, Wing Commander G P Gibson, accompanied by two of his senior officers, Flight Lieutenant J V Hopgood and Squadron Leader H M Young – both of whom were to be amongst the 53 men killed out of the total of 133 who were engaged in the operation, flew a Lancaster bomber over the Derwent Reservoir to test his own ability to fly the aircraft at low levels in bad light. The second was some two weeks later, and no doubt accounts for the entry in Gibson's log book for 9 April that refers to a 'Base – Derwent Reservoir' flight, when the two towers of the Derwent Dam were used to test the triangular wooden bomb-sight that was being developed for use in the raid.

Thus, the role of the Derwent Dam and its impounded reservoir in the preparations for the mission, one of the most ambitious of the Second World War, was somewhat limited. However, the legend has snowballed out of all proportion through local and media hype. Indeed, even when presented with a precis of the facts in the present author's recent book *Walls across the Valley. The Building of the Howden and Derwent Dams*, the reviewer for one local glossy monthly simply reiterated that the book contained 'reminders that here was the testing place of the dambusters'. Factuality was also ignored, either for the sake of convenience or through ignorance, by the organisers of commemorative fly-pasts on 16 May 1977, 2 October 1986, 16 May 1988 and 19 May 1993, which also progressively attracted increasing numbers of a credulous populace.

The use of the dam and its environs as a location in a commercial film released in 1955 effected an early escalation of the local hype, which would appear to have been actively elaborated at least since 1946. In that year the Chairman of the Derwent Valley Water Board reported to the meeting of its Finance and General Purposes Committee on 15 March 'that he had received a letter [see Note 2] from Lady Riverdale [one of the local 'titles'] asking whether the Board would consider naming some part of the Board's Works [the formal inauguration of the Ladybower Dam had been effected on the previous 25 September] after Wing Commander Guy Gibson, VC, who had led the Air Squadron in the attack on the Moehne and Eder Dams'. The committee resolved accordingly 'That the Clerk be instructed to write Lady Riverdale and inform her that the Committee had given very careful and sympathetic consideration to the suggestion, but there appeared to be no part of the Board's Works which was available and could be appropriately named after this distinguished Airman. It was agreed, however, that the Board would bear Lady Riverdale's suggestion in mind in the event of any work being constructed by the Board in the future which could be appropriately named after him'. Fortunately nothing was – a providential sequel indeed, for the association of Gibson's name with what is largely a local fallacy would have been unbefitting to the memory of such a brave young man.

It seems that what has happened at Derwent is that local sentiment just got in on the act – leading to a memorial on the dam and so forth – and the credulity of the populace has done the rest. Perhaps the locals involved should be rewarded for their enterprise, but definitely not at the expense of the truth, for 'facts do not cease to exist because they are ignored' (Aldous Huxley (1894-1963), *Proper Studies* (1927), 'Note on Dogma'). Nevertheless, although the role of the Derwent Dam and Reservoir in the Dambusters' practice programme was rather restricted, the dam's physical resemblance to the Moehne Dam does make it, as a visual symbol, as good a memorial as any to that unique and courageous exploit. A venture in which 53 young airmen of the 133 involved lost their lives.

BIBLIOGRAPHY

'A Lost Village is Recalled' in *South Yorkshire Times*, 29 November 1975, p.55 (see also 4 September 1976 and 5 February 1977).

Birchinlee, the Workmen's Village of the Derwent Valley Water Board, by Brian Robinson (1983).

'Derbyshire. Submerged Village. Birchin Lee Reappears in Derwent Reservoir. 14 Years Under Water', in *Sheffield Daily Telegraph*, 18 October 1928.

'High Level Conflict. Divided views on Derwent's role in dams mission', Special report by Roger Green in *Derbyshire Times*, 29 April 1993, pages 8 and 9 (the lead from which this report developed, namely Dr Sweetman's book, was brought to Mr Green's attention, in January 1993, by the author of the present article).

Moorland Heritage, by James S Byford (1981).

The Dams Raid: Epic or Myth. Operation Chastise, by John Sweetman (Jane's Publishing, 1982); a revised, second edition, entitled 'The Dambusters Raid', was published in 1990 by Arms and Armour Press.

The Derwent Valley Water Board: Minutes of Proceedings of the Board, from November 1945 to November 1946, page 21, and the *Commentary on Agenda for Meeting of the Finance and General Purposes Committee to be held at the Council House, Nottingham, 15th March 1946*.

The Railway Navvies, by Terry Coleman (Pelican Books, 1968, 1969, 1970).

Walls Across the Valley. The Building of the Howden and Derwent Dams, by Brian Robinson (Scarthin Books, 1993).

Note 1: Birchinlee must not be confused with the former villages of Derwent (Figures 7 and 8) and Ashopton (Figures 9 and 10), some two and three miles, respectively, southward down the Derwent Valley. These were, indeed, demolished and submerged below the rising waters of the Ladybower Reservoir during 1943-44, although the site and ruins of Derwent and of Derwent Hall to its immediate north have been subsequently occasionally revealed for brief periods as the reservoir's level has fallen accordingly.

However, even this scenario sometimes attracts mis-reporting by the media when it ascribes the roof of the shell of the redundant valve house, which stood immediately across the River Derwent from the village and which is the first significant remaining artifact to appear above the reservoir's surface as its level falls, as the roof of the former village church.

Note 2: The letter reads:
Riverdale Grange SHEFFIELD

19th February 1946

Dear Sir Albert Atkey,
It is possible that you have read Wing Commander Guy Gibson's book "Enemy Coast Ahead". It contains the account of, among other marvellous achievements, the very hazardous training over the valley lakes in this district for the breaching of the Mohne and Eder dams. For this he received his VC, gazetted, I believe, the same day he visited Sheffield in May 1943 for the National Savings 'Wings for Victory' weeks, staying the night with us.

It occurs to me whether it would be possible to name one of the lakes, embankments or roads by his name – The Guy Gibson... as a fitting memorial gesture to one of the most outstanding exploits of the war, and which he led after severe experiments with such splendid skill and daring.

Hoping you may receive my suggestion favourably,

Yours sincerely,

(Sgd)... Frances Riverdale

CHAPTER 8

Blue John
The Myths And The Facts

by P R Ineson

LOCALS WILL CLAIM THAT THE MINERAL THEY CALL Blue John is the rarest natural formation in the British Isles whose only known deposit in the world lies in a hill situated approximately one mile west of the Derbyshire village of Castleton. They will continue to relate how the name was given to it by two miners, John Kirk and Joseph Hall, in the eighteenth century, in order to distinguish it from 'Black Jack', the local name for Zinc Blend, and how during excavations at Pompeii two vases made from Blue John were unearthed, evidence that the Romans not only discovered the mineral at Castleton nearly 2,000 years ago but also appreciated it for its ornamental value. As to the cause of the mineral's many varied colours, they are less sure, but may suggest that it is reasonable to suppose that intrusive substances, such as mineral oxides or hydrocarbons in the form of mineral oils, are responsible. Such is the tale, but what is factuality?

Who first used/called the mineral 'Blue John'?
Blue John is a variety of fluorite and one of the early records, from Germany, uses the term *flusspath*. This may relate to its fluxing properties which were known in the sixteenth century. In 1700, Charles Leigh's *Natural History of Lancashire, Cheshire and Derbyshire* mentioned the occurrence of 'sappherene and Azure Spar', which may refer to Blue John, but it was not until the 1750s and 1760s that the word Blue John was used.

We do not know who first coined the term. There is no early documentary evidence for the claim that Castleton miners John Kirk and Joseph Hall first used the term Blue John in 1770 to distinguish it from Black Jack (the zinc ore, sphalerite). However, it is certain that when, around 1765, Matthew

Boulton of Birmingham was manufacturing ormulu ornaments with the gilt work on a core of polished stones or porcelain, he called the stone 'Blew John' and, indeed, it became such a popular base for the ornaments that he tried to lease the whole output of the mines.

The earliest dated decorative application of Blue John is its use in marble fireplace panels designed by Robert Adam and installed in Kedleston Hall near Derby in 1762. Around this date the stone must have been known nationally and this may also coincide with the rebuilding of Chatsworth House and its commensurate use in the numerous marble works being set up in Derbyshire. One of the paramount figures of the time who 'worked' Blue John was Henry Watson who, in partnership with John Platt, owned and extracted Blue John from the Treak Cliff mines. Some of the Blue John was sent to France for gilding by the French ormulu workers of the Louis XVI period and this may be the derivation of another suggestion as to its name. Blue John may be the corruption of the French description 'bleu et jaune' (blue and yellow). However, no connection is known except for the ormulu workers who may have copied Matthew Boulton's lead in its use.

Did the Romans export Blue John vases back to Italy?
This is most probably a myth. William Adam's book *The Gem of the Peak* reported Blue John vases being found at Pompeii. Adam, a spar and marble manufacturer and dealer in Matlock Bath, may well have reported the find as good 'sales talk' when, in the 1840s, interest in classical countries was much in vogue. Furthermore, Blue John has never been located by archaeologists from a Roman site in Britain and, likewise, there is no evidence for Roman mining in Castleton.

Pliny, describing all the precious stones known to the Romans, notes a stone which resembles Blue John. It formed the Vasa Murrhina and Pliny records that it came from Parthia and Carmania which were provinces in Southern Persia (now Iran). More recently, two cups of a blue-and-yellow-banded fluorspar were found in a Roman grave near the Turkish-Syrian border. As this locality is en route between Southern Iran and Rome, it may be close to one of the then trade routes.

Does Blue John only occur at Castleton?
Blue John is a variety of fluorite. Fluorite (calcium fluoride, CaF_2) is the mineral while fluorspar is the name given to the fluorite ore which is mined, subsequently processed and used industrially. Pure fluorite is colourless and transparent, but

varieties occur in almost every colour, with common colours of yellow, blue to purple and black, pale and dark red and the rare pale to mid-green. Of all these varieties, the Blue John found at Castleton is the best known, no doubt due to its use in antique ornaments, its sale as jewellery and small ornaments, especially bowls, and visits to the show caves/mines by the public. Blue John is not a gem, nor a precious stone, but may be considered to be a semi-precious stone because of its beauty and rarity rather than its hardness and durability.

Blue fluorite occurs widely throughout Derbyshire and especially in the Ashover and Crich areas. It also occurs where other fluorspar deposits have been mined and so may be found in County Durham (especially Weardale), Cornwall and Wales as well as throughout the world. The Blue John at Castleton consists of radiating crystalline masses which display various patterns and intensities of blue to purple bands alternating with white, yellow or reddish bands. It is this banding which is the characteristic feature of Blue John. It is found in open joints, ancient caves and voids in a boulder bed at Treak Cliff and alternating patterns are known locally as fourteen 'veins' which are mined (during the winter when the show caves are closed to visitors) and used to make the various pieces for sale in Castleton and surrounding villages and towns.

The deposits of Blue John at Castleton have been regarded as unique, although unfortunately similar banded blue and white fluorite is now being imported from China. It is being cut and polished and sold as coming from Castleton and only an expert can tell the difference. Additional localities where such deposits occur are in Nevada (in the USA) and Southern Iran, but, as of today (1993/4), this material has not found its way into the UK market.

What is the origin of the blue and white banding in the mineral?
There have been a number of theories proposed as to the origin of the colouration in Blue John. Certain of these have been tested, but it is doubtful if the correct reason has yet been advocated and, indeed, the controversy continues to be investigated. Itemised below are the majority of the theories which have been favoured.

(i) The banding is due to the inclusion of traces of a mineral containing manganese. Analysis has disproved this, for no variations in the manganese content between the colour bands were noted.

(ii) Organic matter is present in the Blue John and this is said to be responsible for the colour banded variations; extracting and identifying the responsible organic compounds has, so far, failed to provide a definite conclusion.

(iii) The colour bands are related to deposition from fluids at different temperatures. There is no evidence for this.

(iv) The colour is related to an excess of calcium in colloidal form, and heating a sample causes a loss in colour (? by dispersing the colloidal calcium). It may be reinstated, but the technique is comparable to hitting a nut with a sledgehammer, for the samples have to be bombarded in an atomic pile, when, it is claimed, new lattice distortions are created.

(v) Molecular lattice distortions giving rise to colour variations have also been related to radiation from the surrounding rocks which contain radio-active elements.

(vi) The colour is an optical effect of the lattice distortions, and these may relate to uraniferous radiation damage or uranium absorbed onto the organic inclusions. The surrounding shales – the Edale Shales – around Castleton are uranium-bearing and have been said to be responsible for the high radon levels in the cellars of some of the houses in the area. Four types of inclusions have been recorded in Blue John, but they could not be correlated with specific colours.

(vii) Another study has examined the cleavage flakes of Blue John and could not find any inclusions of either an organic or uraniferous type, nor were dislocations in the crystals between different colours noted. It was proposed that while the individual crystals were growing (at irregular rates), organic matter and possibly uranium may have been deposited for a short period of time only, to be flushed away (redissolved) by a subsequent influx of fluoride-bearing solutions. This may explain the banding as due to the intermittent formation of a colloidal calcium metal lattice which was virtually identical to that of the fluorite. Why this process should give rise to blue, purple or white colours is difficult to comprehend.

(viii) If colourless fluorite is bombarded with X-rays (or an electron beam), a blue to purple colouration is produced in the crystal. However, the colour was not permanent and faded with time.

It is clear that at the present time the origin of the colour banding of Blue John remains unresolved.

BIBLIOGRAPHY

Atkinson, P (1983) *A fluid inclusion study and geochemical investigation of the fluorite deposits of the South Pennines.* Ph.D. thesis, University of Leicester.

Blount, B and Sequira, J A (1919) 'Blue John and other forms of fluorite', in *Journal of the Chemical Society and Transactions*, **115**, pp.705-709.

Braithwaite, R S W, Flowers, W T, Haszeldine, R N and Russell, M (1973) 'The cause of the colour of Blue John and other purple fluorites', in *Mineralogical Magazine*, **39**, pp.401-411.

Carruthers,, R G and Pocock, R W (1922) 'Fluorspar', *Geological Survey Special Report on the Mineral Resources of Great Britain*, **4**, 2nd edition, 42pp.

Dickson, J A D (1980) 'Artificial colouration of fluorite by electron bombardment', in *Mineralogical Magazine*, **43**, pp.820-822.

Dunham, K C (1937) 'The paragenesis and colour of fluorite in the English Pennines', in *American Mineralogist*, **22**, pp.468-478.

Dunham, K C (1952) 'Fluorspar', in *Geological Survey Special Reports on Mineral Resources*, **4**, 4th edition, 143pp.

Ford, T D (1955) 'Blue John Fluorspar', in *Proceedings of the Yorkshire Geological Society*, **30**, pp.35-60.

Ford, T D (1962) 'Recent studies of mineral distribution in Derbyshire and their significance', in *Bulletin of the Peak District Mines Historical Society*, **1**, (5), pp.3-9.

Ford, T D (1969) 'The Blue John fluorspar deposits of Treak Cliffe, Derbyshire, in relation to the Boulder Bed', in *Proceedings of the Yorkshire Geological Society*, **37**, pp.153-157.

Ford, T D (1979) 'Blue John: Derbyshire's unique gem', in *Gems Magazine*, **11**, (2), pp.13-23.

Ford, T D and Rieuwerts, J H (1976) 'Odin Mine, Castleton, Derbyshire', in *Bulletin of the Peak District Mines Historical Society*, **6**, (4), 54pp.

Ford, T D and Sarjeant, W A S (1964) 'The Peak District Mineral Index', in *Bulletin of the Peak District Mines Historical Society*, **2**, pp.122-150.

Galway, A K, Jones, K A, Reed, R and Dollimore, D (1979) 'The blue colouration in banded fluorite (Blue John) from Castleton, Derbyshire', in *Mineralogical Magazine*, **43**, pp.243-250.

Garnett, C S (1920) 'Colouring matters of red and blue fluorites', in *Journal of the Chemical Society Transactions*, **117**, p.620.

Holgate, N (1973) 'Dichroic pigment layers in Blue John fluorite', in *Mineralogical Magazine*, **39**, pp.363-366.

Howie, R A, Pegram, E and Walsh, J N (1982) 'The content of rare earths in English fluorites: a preliminary study', in *Journal of the Russell Society*, **1**, pp.22-25.

Mackenzie, K J D and Green, J M (1971) 'The cause of the colouration in Derbyshire Blue John banded fluorite and other blue banded fluorites', in *Mineralogical Magazine*, **38**, pp.459-470.

Mason, J E (1974) 'The geology of Derbyshire fluorspar deposits', pp.10-22 in: *A Symposium on the Geology of Fluorspar*. Special Publication of the Kentucky Geological Survey, Series X, **22**, 107pp.

Mueller, G (1954) 'The distribution of the coloured varieties of fluorites in the thin thermal zones of the Derbyshire mineral deposits'. 19th International Geological Congress, Algiers; *Compte Rendu, Fasc.*, **15**, pp.523-539.

Pering, K L (1973) 'Bitumens associated with lead, zinc and fluorite ore minerals in North Derbyshire, England', in *Geochimica et Cosmochimica Acta*, **37**, pp.401-417.

Rogers, P J (1977) 'Fluid inclusion studies in fluorite from the Derbyshire orefield', in *Transactions of the Institute of Mining & Metallurgy, Section B*, **B86**, pp.B128-132.

Stevenson, D P and Gaunt, G D (1971) 'The geology of the country around Chapel-en-le-Frith' in *Memoirs of the Geological Survey of GB*. 430pp.

Stokes, A H (1899) 'Castleton history, geology, minerals and mining', in *Transactions of the Institute of Mining Engineers*, **18**, pp.266-278.

Wedd, C D and Drabble, G C (1908) 'The fluorspar deposits of Derbyshire', in *Transactions of the Institute of Mining Engineers*, **35**, pp.501-535.

CHAPTER 9

Dorothy Vernon's Elopement
Fact Or Fiction?

by Brian Robinson

THE CASUAL VISITOR TO HADDON HALL LEAVES with a mind well primed with the tale of the elopement of Dorothy Vernon, the younger daughter of Sir George Vernon and a co-heiress to the estate, with John Manners, the second son of the Earl of Rutland. This story of oppression, merry-making, a beautiful young woman, love, flight, galloping horses and, (the usual termination of such a sequence of events), a secret marriage followed by paternal forgiveness, is of little consequence, be it fact or fiction. Nonetheless, for many decades this tale of the fair Derbyshire Juliet and her Romeo has titillated the minds of credulous tourists, given Dorothy, who would otherwise have remained largely unknown, the status of a local celebrity and introduced an element of romance into the foundation of the Manners' dynasty at Haddon.

This affair is supposed to have taken place in 1563, or thereabouts, although some versions claim 1558 as the date. So far as can be ascertained, however, it was not given literary birth until 1822 when, in March, *The London Magazine* carried an anonymous article entitled 'The King of the Peak, a Derbyshire Tale'. Later in that year the story was reprinted (with alterations) in *Tales of the English and Scottish Peasantry*, by Allan Cunningham.

In Cunningham's account of the elopement, the heroine is throughout called Dora Vernon, the couple taking flight from Haddon during a hunting feast at which Manners is disguised as a minstrel, and no mention is made of their wedding. His sources of the tale are the 'ancient portress' of the Hall and an 'old husbandman' of 70 years who were, in fact, characters well known at this time as guides to the building. The old man was William Hague who, together with his wife, played a considerable

Figure 1. The so-called 'Dorothy Vernon's Steps' and 'Dorothy Vernon's Door' at Haddon Hall (from Jewitt, p.36).

role in making Haddon popular with sightseers. He died in 1840 – being buried at Bakewell on the 9th of May that year – having for upward of half a century conducted visitors over Haddon Hall. That the Dorothy Vernon story was part of their stock-in-trade seems obvious, but where did the story originate? Cunningham's old husbandman gives his great-great-grandfather as his authority, and there is good evidence for Hague's family's long association with Haddon and the Manners family. It would appear that the portress, too, came from a local family. This combination of facts suggests that the story was an old local tradition, but whether there was any truth in it remains to be determined.

A year later, in 1823, the tale is referred to by John Holland in his *Haddon Hall, a Poetical Sketch* – in this work, the same 'ancient portress' features as the guide and, although it is quite likely that Holland had read Cunningham's account, it can hardly be doubted that his verses record an actual visit he paid to Haddon from his home in nearby Sheffield.

Also in 1823 the yarn appeared in the more sumptuous guise of a three-volume novel, *The King of the Peak*, the author of which assumed the name of Lee Gibbons. William Bennett, alias Lee Gibbons, who visited the district in February 1822 and explains in his preface that he was contemplating writing the novel before he read the article on the same subject in *The London Magazine* in 1822, also declares he had the whole tale from the then custodian of the Hall. In his version, Dorothy Vernon flees by a window, leaving a slipper behind her in the act – shades of pantomime? The book ends hastily with the prospect of a double marriage of the two sisters.

Since then, via the publication of several more novels and novelettes, a play and a film story, the legend has become further embellished.

As now told, it divides up as follows:

(i) Dorothy Vernon, an heiress but only second daughter, falls in love with the second son of the Earl of Rutland, John Manners, apparently a resourceful lover.

(ii) Whilst her elder sister, Margaret, has an open attachment to Sir Thomas Stanley, the son of the Earl of Derby, and is made much of, Dorothy is kept in the background and plays a definite second fiddle. When her secret attachment to Manners is discovered, it is opposed by her father, sister and step-mother, the lover is forbidden to enter the house, and she is closely watched and kept almost a prisoner.

(iii) Manners, with the resource naturally to be looked for in the resolute and devoted lover of ancient times, disguises himself as a woodman, or forester, and remains in hiding in the woods around Haddon for several weeks, in order to obtain stolen glances of and occasional brief meetings with Dorothy.

(iv) Dorothy is eventually unable to endure her situation and the oppression of her step-mother any longer and, during a feast and ball (sometimes depicted as the wedding feast of her sister, Margaret) she flies to her lover, whose open arms are waiting for her by the nearby footbridge.

(v) Horses are waiting and the beautiful maiden and her lover ride off into the moonlight.

(vi) The pair, after an all-night ride, reach Aylestone, near Leicester, where they are duly married.

However, vital aspects of this scenario do not survive scrutiny.

(a) The rejection by the family of Manners as a suitor is difficult to comprehend. Why should this powerful country squire, Sir George Vernon, have been so bitterly opposed to his younger daughter becoming the wife of the second son of so mighty an earl as the Earl of Rutland? As a match, viewed from the standpoint of social advantage, it was in all aspects desirable and excellent. In what lies the cause of complaint? The religious question has been made the whipping-boy. However, in those days, differences of religious views and opinions were as much a matter of politics as of doctrine and seldom stood in the way of a desirable marriage.

(b) In the story, Dorothy has a step-mother. But had she at the time of the alleged elopement, if we accept the version that claims it took place on the night of her sister's wedding in 1558? Dorothy's own mother died on 25 March 1558; had her father married for a second time between then and the date of his elder daughter's wedding in the same year? And, if so, had the cruelty of his second wife, in such a short time, driven her younger step-daughter to flight with her lover? It seems most unlikely. Furthermore, whether Sir George's second wife bore her ill-will in later years would appear to be open to considerable doubt, for in her will, she, Mathilda, surrendered to Margaret and Thomas Stanley, and to Dorothy and John Manners, all her interest under the will of her husband in all his possessions. Enmity and hatred, if they ever existed, were most certainly then forgotten.

(c) Le Blanc Smith establishes that in 1565 Dorothy Manners (by this time she was married) was 20 years old, data corroborated by the fact that she was 39 years old when she died in 1584. Thus, if she eloped in 1558, she was at the time only 13 years old. Hardly credible. Furthermore, she then rides on horseback all night – and after a dance – to Aylestone, a distance of some sixty miles, and is there married. The concept of this scenario for a child of 13 years of age is absurd. On the other hand, in other versions of the tale, the event is supposed to have taken place in, or about, 1563, and in Cunningham's account the feast is a hunting feast (not the wedding feast of her sister), with Manners disguised as a minstrel. This dating is certainly more plausible.

(d) And what of the so-called 'Dorothy Vernon's Steps' (Figure 1) down which she is reputed to have escaped? This facet of the tale first appears in print in 1860 when another recruit – one of the earliest of a veritable legion – to the ranks of Dorothy Vernon romanticists, Miss Eliza Meteyard, writing under the nom-de-plume of 'Silverpen', published 'The Love Steps of Dorothy Vernon' in Vol 1 of *The Reliquary*. However, the accounts relating to the building of these steps show that they were not built until 1650, *66 years after Dorothy's death*. Furthermore, there is also considerable doubt that the actual ballroom, at least as a habitable room, was in existence at the time of the imaginary elopement. Nonetheless, the steps and the ballroom still feature in the legend.

(e) Aylestone, in Leicestershire, the ultimate destination of the alleged elopers of our tale, came also to be regarded as the scene of their reputed secret wedding. However, such was not a necessary sequel – indeed, none of the early accounts of the tale suggests that the elopement ended in a runaway marriage – and, in any case, since Aylestone was, like Haddon, one of Sir George Vernon's manors, it would therefore be an unlikely venue for such an event. As a matter of history, John Manners

Figure 2. The monument of Sir John Manners and his wife, Dorothy, which surmounts their tomb in Bakewell Church (from Jewitt, p.61).

undeniably married Dorothy Vernon and became lord of Haddon, in right of his wife, following Sir George Vernon's death. However, no reference to, or details of, their marriage are extant in the apposite parish registers. Those for Aylestone commence in 1561, but record no Manners-Vernon wedding (as might have resulted from an elopement in 1563, or thereabouts), whereas those for Bakewell, the most likely venue for their wedding in normal circumstances, do not exist for the period, neither in the original nor the bishop's transcripts.

(f) Finally, what of the personal appearance of the 'fair and lovely Dorothy'? According to former guide books to Haddon Hall, 'it is said that she was one of the most beautiful of all beautiful women, and possessed of so sweet a temper that she was idolised by all who knew her'. However, such is far from substantiated by her monument, which accompanies that of her husband on their tomb in Bakewell Church (Figure 2). It portrays her as being far from either amiable or attractive, although it has been suggested, once again without any evidence, that this representation may not be a truthful portrait.

An attempt to support the legend of the elopement may be sought in the old adage 'Where there is smoke there is fire'. However, what is this smoke? History knows it not, for it contains no documentary evidence whatsoever, emanating, together with all its irregularities, entirely from the local anecdotal hearsay handed down through several generations of a family who acted as retainers to the Manners household and who used it as stock-in-trade banter for tourists. The plethora of damning evidence to the contrary outlined above has been available in the literature since 1908, when it was concluded that 'enough now has surely been said to prove that Dorothy Vernon's love tale must be considered as one of romance only – one of those fables, indeed, which has grown up, as fables always will grow up, around stately homes and prominent personages'. Nevertheless, the tale lingers on as actuality.

Perhaps that well-known scholar of Derbyshire's history, the late Dr J C Cox, writing in 1907, should be permitted the final word. 'Haddon appeals to all sorts and conditions of men. Its romantic situation and venerable appearance delight the ordinary sightseer; its veritable and unrestored antiquity appeals to the more earnest student of bygone ways; while to those interested in the minute details of the past, it is a store-house of all kinds of work wrought in all kinds of styles. Surely, it has enough of true and genuine interest to be able to dispense with the fictitious, sixpenny-magazine romance of Dorothy Vernon. Let those who cling to her invented story, and picture her as a fascinating, winsome heroine, go and look at her portraiture on her monument in Bakewell Church – a more staid, prosaic person could hardly be imagined'.

BIBLIOGRAPHY

Memorials of Old Derbyshire ed. by J Charles Cox (Bemrose, London and Derby; 1907), p.136.

'Dorothy Vernon, Heiress of Haddon', by G Le Blanc Smith, in *Journal of the Derbyshire Archaeological and Natural History Society*, 1908, **30**, pp.97-102.

The Illustrated History and Guide to Haddon Hall, by Llewellyn Jewitt (Heywood, Manchester), pp.11, 12.

Dorothy Vernon's Elopement. Tale or Tradition?, Local History Leaflet, No 3 (Department of Local History and Archives, Sheffield City Libraries, 1955 – revised 1960).

'Dorothy Vernon's Elopement. Tale or Tradition?', in *Sheffield Spectator*, 1969, **9**, No 53 (September).

'Did Dorothy Vernon Elope?', in *A Sheaf of Essays by a Sheffield Antiquary*, the late Charles Drury, Essay XXXI, pp.138-140.

CHAPTER 10

For Arkwright Read Lombe?

by Harry E Butterton

MARKET FORCES APPARENTLY RULED SUPREME even at the dawn of the industrial age. Perhaps that is what it has all been about, all along! Richard Arkwright's Cromford is commonly taken to be the first powerhouse of the modern world with the magic ingredient, his water-frame, in the judgment of his most recent biographer, the principal agent in the reconstitution of the work-surface of England. However, there is still no agreement, it seems, on whether he actually invented the machine! In this tiny community, at the exit of a rocky gorge of the River Derwent, the modern factory system by common repute started; shift-working, mass-production and all.

There is no denying Arkwright's real gifts were those of the entrepreneur, for the putting up of cotton mills, for ensuring that the factory system would be the norm for the working life of the future and for creating the mass market for big-scale production and consumption of cheap cotton goods. But in reality, when Cromford's first mill was constructed in 1771, another mill, likewise water-powered beside the same River Derwent, was already a full half-century old. The Old Silk Mill at Derby (Figure 1), the building of which was begun in 1718 and completed in 1722, as the creation of John and Thomas Lombe and their engineer George Sorocold, is described by the eminent modern art-historian Francis Klingender as 'the first large manufactory in England'. Almost a quarter of a century before the first Cromford structure raised its five storeys skyward, an unpublished Latin poem of 1748 by a Scots cleric, the Reverend James Gatt, minister of Gretna, included this ecstatic passage:

'Are not the discoveries of men worthy of celebration? Who can sufficiently admire this unique work? Your silk-mill, Derby, is constructed with such skill that in my judgment it is certain that nothing finer has been found in the whole world. Who, standing beside it, is not astounded by so many movements, and

as many wheels, and the brilliance of mind by which such a machine was produced?'

Moreover, as we shall see, that wonder of the early eighteenth century was not even the first industrial structure on that very same site almost within the afternoon shadow of All Saints' Church.

Of course, silk could not have the mass-market possibilities and appeal of cheap cotton products. Nevertheless, perhaps the comparative repute of the Old Derby Silk Mill has suffered at least in part because the Arkwright phenomenon coincided with, of all things, a heightened artistic consciousness towards the end of the eighteenth century. The Cromford mills now lie enshrined in the poetry of that busy intellectual country doctor from Lichfield, Erasmus Darwin, and hung in nocturnal splendour by that superlative Derby artist, Joseph Wright. At least Darwin's verse might, with almost equal justice, include the by then (1791) antique Derby enterprise in its embrace when he writes:

'So now, where Derwent guides his dusky floods
Through vaulted mountains, and a night of woods...
His ponderous oars to slender spindles turns,
And pours o'er massy wheels his foamy urns...
And slowly circumvolves the labouring wheel below'
- though it must be conceded that Darwin's use of the term 'o'er' is more appropriate to the Cromford overshot as opposed to the Silk Mill undershot waterwheel as the motif of driving

Figure 1. The Lombes' Silk Mill at Derby in 1794 as viewed from the east bank of the River Derwent. The foundation arches, which remain extant as referred to in the text, are clearly visible, as is the tower of the nearby cathedral.

Figure 2. The
original foundation
arches for Lombe's
Silk Mill at Derby
(from Cooper, p.50).

power. It may be, however, that Wright's magical painting,
'Arkwright's Cotton Mills by Night' of about 1782, with every
window alive with candlelight or oil lamp beneath full moon
and scudding cloud, has etched an indelible and potent association between Cromford and the forces of the first industrial
revolution. There is no evidence that Wright painted it on com-
mission. He must simply have been impressed, ignoring the
image of the old Derby mill virtually on his own doorstep just
round the corner from his studio in the county town's Irongate!
Even so, it was probably no accident that he came to be in
Cromford, tucked away in the hills though it was, since he was
to be commissioned to produce his masterly portrait of
Arkwright (1789) – with cotton-spinning rollers beside him as
the foundation of all his bulldog splendour – and in so doing
was to contribute to the Cromford legend.

So the record does need to be straightened. If it is a case of
'firsts' in the modern age, it is the town site that should have it.
Last year, 1993, marked the 275th anniversary, no less, of the
laying of the stone foundation arches of the Derby Silk Mill in
1718 – before either Darwin or Wright had been born!

Figure 3. The Old Silk Mill gates, made by Robert Bakewell about 1722 and now re-erected on their original site (from Cooper, p.45).

Admittedly, much less is left to us today (Figures 2 to 4) of its original appearance than is the case at Arkwright's Cromford, where the all-important driving water-channel can still be viewed. Yet those Sorocold foundation arches are still there (Figure 2) beside the river in the county town. An intrinsic visual distinction that matches the story behind them! For this was indeed an establishment which has a unique claim to fame in the world of modern manufacture. It could be argued that the products of the giants of the English architectural scene in the year 1718, of the likes of Christopher Wren, Hawksmoor and Vanbrugh, were of less relevance to future generations of their countrymen than the building of spare grace then under construction beside the Derwent. This would prove to be the ancestor of all modern factories, the progenitor of the boxed skeletal framework at the heart of modern building design; though it was a lesser-known member of the Strutt textile dynasty who, seventy-five years later in time but only a matter of minutes on foot away in the same busy town, translated the Silk Mill's wood into latter-day metal and constructed a mill with fire-proof iron framework. This forged the final link to Victorian and later building technology. The Silk Mill indeed constituted a unique portent of the factory age, where a new method of industrial production was pioneered based on the efficient tripod of *revolutionary building form, single power source* (water) and *work practice geared to the demands of machinery*.

One modern authority, Dr W J Richardson, explains this aspect of the Derby mill's importance:

'The Silk Mill was not merely an engineering wonder but a social phenomenon, almost a portent. Fifty years before the first cotton mill was spinning yarn, here in Derby a population of operatives worked regular hours in a factory, the like of which had not been seen in this country, and the pace of their working was that of machines.'

The mill was important, too, for the national trade and economy of the time. P D Wilde points out that the Old Silk Mill liberated the makers of English silk from crippling dependence on Italy, a judgment backing the writer of the 1827 *Walk Through Derby*:

'Its history is remarkable, as it denotes the power of genius and the vast influence which even the enterprises of an individual have on the commerce of a Country. The Italians were long in the exclusive possession of the art of silk throwing, and the merchants of other nations were consequently dependent on that people for their participation in a very lucrative article of trade, and were frequently deprived of their fair profits by the

exorbitant prices charged for the original material. This state of things continued till the commencement of the last century . . .'

For the town of Derby itself, its importance was enormous, as the compilers of the 1849 Board of Health Report on the town make clear:

'Since the establishment in 1719 [sic] of a silk throwing mill at Derby, by a mechanic and draughtsman named John Lombe, the chief part of the population have been employed in the silk manufacture; the town has in consequence grown up into the importance which it at present enjoys.'

Looking at the whole span of Derby's history and development in the modern era, Dr W J Richardson comes to the conclusion that:

'Not only was the output of spun silk enormously increased, the trade of the town stimulated, a new outlook created, but the tradition of skilled factory working was built up as each successive generation of operatives came into training. This was to benefit the town enormously in the days of the nineteenth century when industry after industry would be attracted to it.'

When the silk trade slipped into decline, engineering would take its place, the one industry building on the experience and expertise of the other. Such a claim cannot remotely be made for the Cromford site.

The founding Royal Patent was granted to John Lombe's half-brother(?) and financier, Thomas, a London merchant, though the family originated in Norfolk. Its wording neatly encapsulates the purpose and hopes invested in it:

'. . . to twist the finest Italian raw silk into organzine in great perfection which was never before done in this our Kingdom, by which means many thousand families of our subjects may be constantly employed in Great Britain, be furnished with silks of all sorts of the manufacture of our subjects, and great quantities exported into foreign parts by being made as good and cheap as any foreign silk can be.'

With silk stockings possibly an even more important, and certainly more apparent, element of men's rather than women's dress in that era following the restoration of the monarchy after the Puritan years, demand for silk yarn was high. Thus it was that sixteen years before the foundation of the Derby Silk Mill by the Lombes, an earlier and much smaller one had been set up on the site in 1702. The entrepreneur was one Thomas Cotchett, a solicitor, born in Mickleover just outside Derby in 1640 who, for some as yet unknown reason, had set himself up as a 'reeler', or supplier of textile equipment, in London after his spell studying Law at Gray's Inn. A member of Cotchett's Derby

Figure 4. The Silk Mill as it exists today (from Cooper, p.44).

workforce was that very John Lombe who, sixteen years later with his half-brother(?) Thomas, would be responsible for the much bigger affair on that very same site.

But why were these factories built in Derby and not in Nottingham? Nottinghamshire had far more hosiery producers in the early 1700s than Derbyshire, and Nottingham was the main market for silk in the East Midlands. What must have attracted both Thomas Cotchett and John Lombe was what, in fact, pulled Arkwright also out of the town by the Trent a century later – though it has been suggested by some that it was frustration with pre-Luddite machine-breakers that really decided the matter for him. It was the availability of water-power from the swift-flowing Derwent, much more suitable than the languid Trent, that was decisive. According to R Lowe's *General view of the agriculture of the county of Nottingham* (1789), silk mills in Nottingham were still being driven by horses, as was Arkwright's first cotton mill there!

The machinery of Italian design which the Lombes would put into their Derby mill was much too big for cottages and would require for its driving the aid of water flowing at speed. Further-more, the Derby Silk Mill would continue to hog the technological edge over Cromford, in that sometime during the first half of the nineteenth century there was a conversion to steam-power, something that never happened on the Cromford site.

But we should never forget the purely human factor. Might it not also have been the presence in the town of a water engineer of genius that clinched the issue of the siting of the silk mill all those years before Cromford was ever heard of in technological circles. For both Cotchett's and the Lombes' mills were built by George Sorocold, probably a Lancastrian by birth, but married at the early age of sixteen at All Saints', looking down on the future industrial site, to the daughter of a Derby apothecary. Sorocold, described by Klingender as one of the earliest millwrights to become a great engineer, had engineered Derby's water supply in 1692. This was powered by a water-wheel set up close to the By-Flatt, just down-river from the silk mill to come, pumping the water through four miles of wooden pipes made of the bored-out trunks of elm trees. The mill for Thomas Cotchett followed in 1702, with the much larger effort for the Lombes completed twenty years later.

Cotchett's 'Old Shop' continued in production side by side with the Lombes' factory almost throughout the century, but eventually had to give way to its monster new relative because its machinery was not a success. However, one modern commentator, Mark Higginson, writes about it that:

'This was probably the first instance where a group of workers were housed under one roof together with machinery and a source of power, and it might therefore be described as "the first factory".'

For the Lombes, Sorocold constructed an undershot water-wheel of Dutch design to power the new mill, which was described by Derby's first historian, William Hutton, as follows:

'This ponderous building stands upon huge piles of oak, from sixteen to twenty feet long, driven close to each other with an engine made for that purpose. Over this solid mass of timber is laid a foundation of stone.'

The structure had an overall length of 249 feet (83m), a width of 39 feet (13m) and, with five storeys, went up to 55 feet (18.3m) in height. It was nearly four times as long, nearly twice as high and half as wide again as Cotchett's mill, with a flat broadly crenellated roofline. The whole new complex stretched 120 yards along the bank and encompassed nearly 40,000 sq ft of working space.

So the Derby Silk Mills were a technological marvel, surely erased in the popular image of the first Industrial Revolution by the fact that it was geared to supplying a restricted, comparatively luxury market in contrast to Cromford's cotton, and stricken by the early death, in 1722, of the genius whose idea it all was, John Lombe. Arkwright lived for twice as long and his enterprise was thus enabled to generate the productive capital that speaks volumes and cultivates lasting legends, not to forget the contribution of literature and art described earlier. However, there is one other factor in the continuation of the Cromford-Arkwright legend, stemming partly from the great mill-owner's comparative longevity. He used some of his great wealth to create one of the celebrated early industrial communities, with workers' housing, a school, and even an hotel to attract visitors and generate fame! It was a recipe to be repeated, varied, and even improved upon at such places as Darley Abbey, a mile up-river from Lombe's site, New Lanark and Saltaire. It was a package that John Lombe never lived long enough to consider, something that attracts the tourist by the thousand even today. Additionally, the Arkwright empire lasted, with Masson Mill, bearing the legend 'Sir Richard Arkwright Est.1769', providing over 200 years of service to industry until its closure in 1993. In contrast, the Derby Silk Mill, which failed to get the patents for its machinery extended when they expired in 1732, was frequently struggling after the death of Sir Thomas Lombe, a mere twenty years after its foundation, and finally ceased production in the 1890s.

John Lombe was like a comet, briefly lighting up the industrial dawn, and providing such a contrast to the solid virtues of the ever-successful Arkwright story; industrial empire and family dynasty. It is time his reputation as the father of the factory system in England was re-established.

BIBLIOGRAPHY

Butterton, Harry: *Silk Mill* (the author, 1991).

Cooper, Brian and Neville: *Transformation of a Valley* (Scarthin Books, 1991).

Egerton, Judy: *Wright of Derby* (Tate Gallery, 1990).

Klingender, Francis D: *Art and the Industrial Revolution* (Paladin Books, 1968).

Richardson, Dr W J: Article in *The Derbyshire Advertiser*, October 1954.

THE END?

New for 1994

The Seven Blunders of the Peak

A fresh look at some Derbyshire legends

edited by Brian Robinson

. . . or Derbyshire de-bunked.

Derbyshire is rich in history and legend, not all based on fact. Seven well-known Derbyshire writers and historians put the record straight.

Did Dorothy Vernon wade across the Wye?'

Was the Eyam plague the mumps?

Is Little John really buried at Hathersage?

ISBN 0 907758 77 0

The Cromford Guide

Freda Bayles and Janet Ede

At last — a long-awaited, concise and comprehensive guide to this historic village.

Based on three walks around the village and the surrounding countryside, *The Cromford Guide* points out the many features of interest past and present in this lively village.

48pp 5 maps + photographs
ISBN 0 907758 76 2

Hardbacks

3,500 COPIES SOLD

Transformation of a Valley

Brian Cooper & Neville Cooper

The lively and scholarly story of the Derwent Valley during the development of mines, mills and other industries. The most readable and authoritative guide to the industrial history of the area.

With maps and 130 photographs of historic sites
Bibliography, index   316pp
ISBN 0 907758 17 7

Derbyshire in the Civil War

Brian Stone

The only single-volume work on the subject. It traces the fighting in Derbyshire and the deeds of Derbyshire men elsewhere, and also looks at the plight of non-combatants and the personal animosities motivating leaders on both sides.

Illustrated, with notes, bibliography and index
157pp ISBN 0 907758 58 4

Robert Bakewell: Artist Blacksmith

S. Dunkerley

Thirty-two pages of colour photographs with opposing pages of commentary form the core of this unique life of the great 18th century craftsman in wrought iron.

Bound in high-quality cloth. With line drawings, gazetteer and index. Limited to 750 signed copies.
112pp ISBN 0 907758 24 X

Family Walks

Each book contains 16 short circular walks for adults and children to enjoy together. The 80-page A5 format includes maps, illustrations and black and white photographs. The maps and easy-to-follow route directions are on facing pages. Additional information includes public transport, pubs and cafes, wet weather alternatives and local attractions.

Family Walks in the Lake District. Barry McKay	ISBN 0 907758 40 1
Family Walks in Mendip, Avalon & Sedgemoor. Nigel Vile	ISBN 0 907758 41 X
Family Walks in Mid Wales. Laurence Main	ISBN 0 907758 27 4
Family Walks in the New Forest. Nigel Vile	ISBN 0 907758 60 6
Family Walks in the North Wales Borderlands. Gordon Emery	ISBN 0 907758 50 9
Family Walks North West Kent. Clive Cutter	ISBN 0 907758 36 3
Family Walks in the North Yorkshire Dales. Howard Beck	ISBN 0 907758 52 5
Family Walks in Oxfordshire. Laurence Main	ISBN 0 907758 38 X
Family Walks in Pembrokeshire. Laurence Main	ISBN 0 907758 75 4
Family Walks in Snowdonia. Laurence Main	ISBN 0 907758 32 0
Family Walks in South Derbyshire. Gordon Ottewell	ISBN 0 907758 61 4
Family Walks around the South Downs. Nick Channer	ISBN 0 907758 73 8
Family Walks in South Gloucestershire. Gordon Ottewell	ISBN 0 907758 33 9
Family Walks in South Shropshire. Marian Newton	ISBN 0 907758 30 4
Family Walks in South Yorkshire. Norman Taylor	ISBN 0 907758 25 8
Family Walks in the Staffordshire Peak & Potteries. Les Lumsdon	ISBN 0 907758 34 7
Family Walks around Stratford & Banbury.	ISBN 0 907758 49 5
Family Walks in Suffolk. C.J. Francis	ISBN 0 907758 64 9
Family Walks in Surrey. Norman Bonney	ISBN 0 907758 74 6
Family Walks around Swansea. Raymond Humphreys	ISBN 0 907758 62 2
Family Walks in the Teme Valley. Camilla Harrison	ISBN 0 907758 45 2
Family Walks in Three Peaks & Malham. Howard Beck	ISBN 0 907758 42 8
Family Walks in Warwickshire. Geoff Allen	ISBN 0 907758 53 3
Family Walks in the Weald of Kent & Sussex. Clive Cutter	ISBN 0 907758 51 7
Family Walks in West London. Caroline Bacon	ISBN 0 907758 72 X
Family Walks in West Yorkshire. Howard Beck	ISBN 0 907758 43 6
Family Walks in the White Peak. Norman Taylor	ISBN 0 907758 09 6
Family Walks in Wiltshire. Nigel Vile	ISBN 0 907758 21 5
Family Walks in the Wye Valley. Heather & John Hurley	ISBN 0 907758 26 6

NEW EXTRA LARGE SIZE

Family Walks around Bakewell and Castleton

Norman Taylor

The same well-loved Family Walks format, enlarged to 96 pages.

ISBN 0 907758 70 3

The Black and White Village Trail

David Gorvett and Les Lumsdon

A 62-mile circular walk in Herefordshire, between Leominster and Kingston, and includes 8 short walks around villages along the way. An adaptation of the Family Walks format.

64pp ISBN 0 907758 47 9

Local History

A popular series of paperbacks, all copiously illustrated with photographs, line drawings or fascimilies.

Our Village
Alison Uttley's Cromford
Alison Uttley

Cromford, well known as the site of the world's first water-powered cotton mill, is also fortunate to have as its chronicler the celebrated essayist and children's writer, Alison Uttley. This collection of essays vividly recalls scenes from the self-sufficient late Victorian village of her childhood. Illustrated by C.F. Tunnicliffe.

72pp ISBN 0 907758 08 8

The Crich Tales
Unexpurgated Echoes from a Derbyshire Village
Geoffrey Dawes

Tales of earthy humour and rural shrewdness, told in a village pub. Illustrations by Geoff Taylor.

96pp ISBN 0 907758 06 1

Hanged for a Sheep
Crime in Bygone Derbyshire
E.G. Power

A factual and entertaining survey of crime and the fight against it from 1750 to 1850.

80pp ISBN 0 907758 00 2

St John's Chapel, Belper
The Life of a Church and a Community
E.G. Power

The history of "The Foresters' Chapel" and the people it served, from the 13th century to the present. This book is not a guidebook for the antiquarian, but easy reading for anyone interested in the past life of Belper and the place of St John's Chapel in that life.

40pp ISBN 0 907758 11 8

Pauper's Venture: Children's Fortune
The Lead Mines and Miners of Brassington

A study of the lead mining community of Brassington. With gazetteer of sites.

52pp ISBN 0 907758 18 5

SPECIAL PRICE

Ancient Wells and Springs of Derbyshire

Peter J. Naylor

The only book on the natural waters of Derbyshire.

80pp ISBN 0 907758 01 0

Journey from Darkness

Gordon Ottewell

A story for older children, set in the mines and countryside of Victorian Derbyshire. It follows the adventures of a pit-boy with his lame pony, escaping the brutality of work to reach an uncle who needs, and can offer, help.

96pp ISBN 0 907758 02 9

Salad Days in Sutton

Charles W. Sanderson

Childhood and youth in Sutton-in-Ashfield between the Wars. Contemporary photographs and drawings by the author.

66pp ISBN 0 907758 14 2

Historical Monographs

A large-format paperback series, well-designed and illustrated with photographs, maps, diagrams and facsimile documents.

Waterways to Derby
A study of the Derwent Navigation and Derby Canal

Celia M. Swainson

The battle to link Derby to the arteries of trade during the Industrial Revolution.

64pp ISBN 0 907758 59 2

Historic Farmhouses around Derby

Barbara Hutton

A detailed study of the old brick and timber farmhouses of South Derbyshire and the Trent Valley.

Full gazetteer/index
64pp ISBN 0 907758 48 7

Millclose: the Mine that Drowned

Lynn Willies, Keith Gregory, Harry Parker

The story of Britain's largest-ever lead mine and the men who worked it.

59 illustrations
64pp ISBN 0 907758 28 2

The publishers welcome suggestions for further titles, and will be pleased to consider manuscripts relating to Derbyshire from new or established authors.

Scarthin Books of Cromford, in the Peak District, are also leading second-hand and antiquarian booksellers, and are eager to purchase specialised material, both ancient and modern.

Contact Dr D.J. Mitchell, 01629-823272.